Best Bush, Coast & Village Walks of The Illawarra

By
Gillian & John Souter

WOODSLANE

Woodslane Press Pty Ltd
Unit 7/5 Vuko Place
Warriewood, NSW 2102
Australia
Email: info@woodslane.com.au
Tel: (02) 9970 5111 Fax: (02) 9970 5002 www.travelandoutdoor.bookcentre.com.au

First published in Australia in 2010 by Woodslane Press

National Library of Australia Cataloguing-in-Publication entry

Author:	Souter, Gillian, 1962-
Title:	Best bush, coast & village walks of the Illawarra : the full-colour guide to over 40 fantastic walks / Gillian Souter, John Souter.
Edition:	1st ed.
ISBN:	9781921606922 (pbk.)
Notes:	Includes index.
Subjects:	Trails--New South Wales--Illawarra Region--Guidebooks. Walking--New South Wales--Illawarra Region. Illawarra (N.S.W.)--Guidebooks. Illawarra (N.S.W.)--Description and travel.
Other Authors/ Contributors:	Souter, John, 1956-
Dewey Number:	919.446

Printed in China by APOL
Designed by Jenny Cowan

Best Bush, Coast & Village Walks of The Illawarra

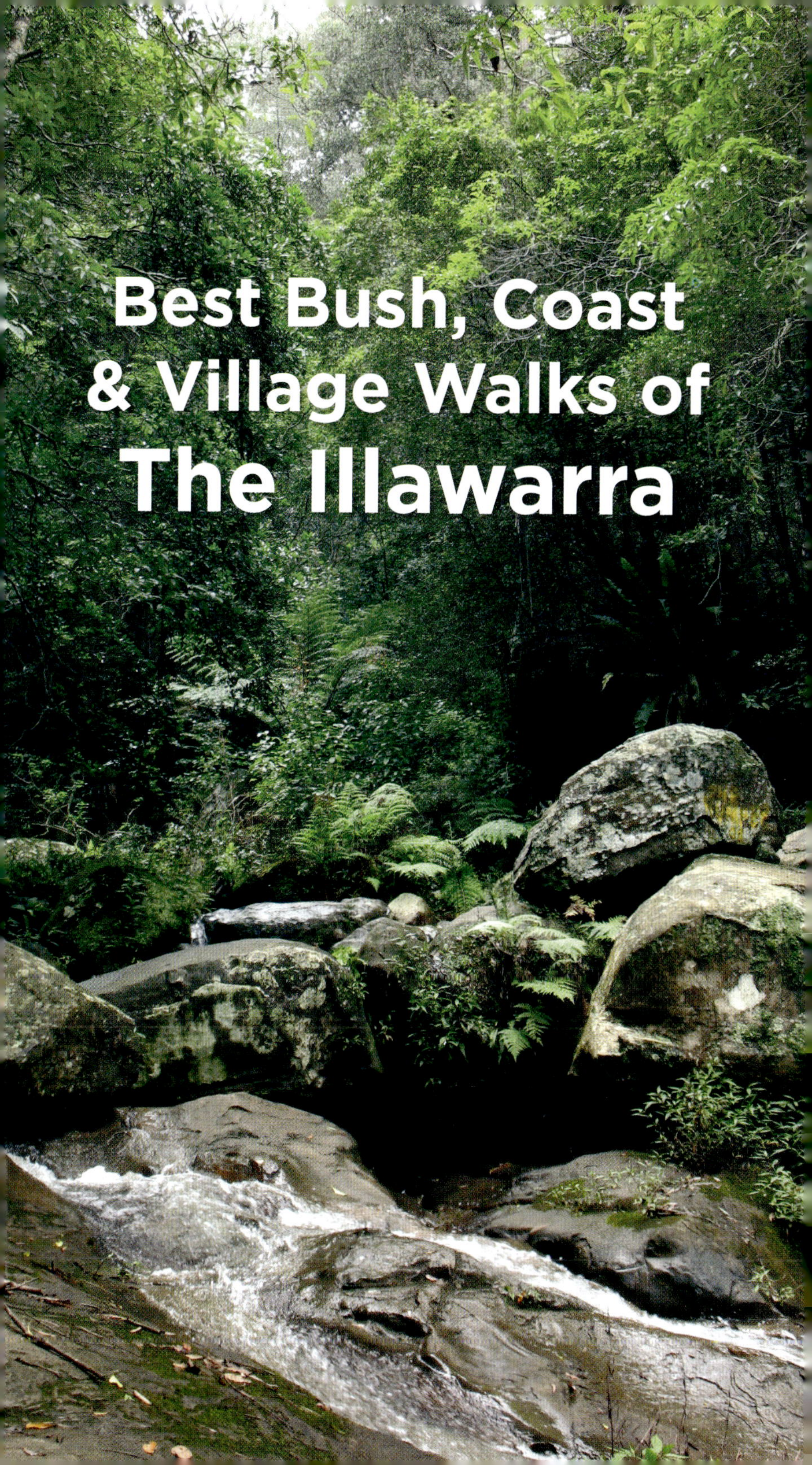

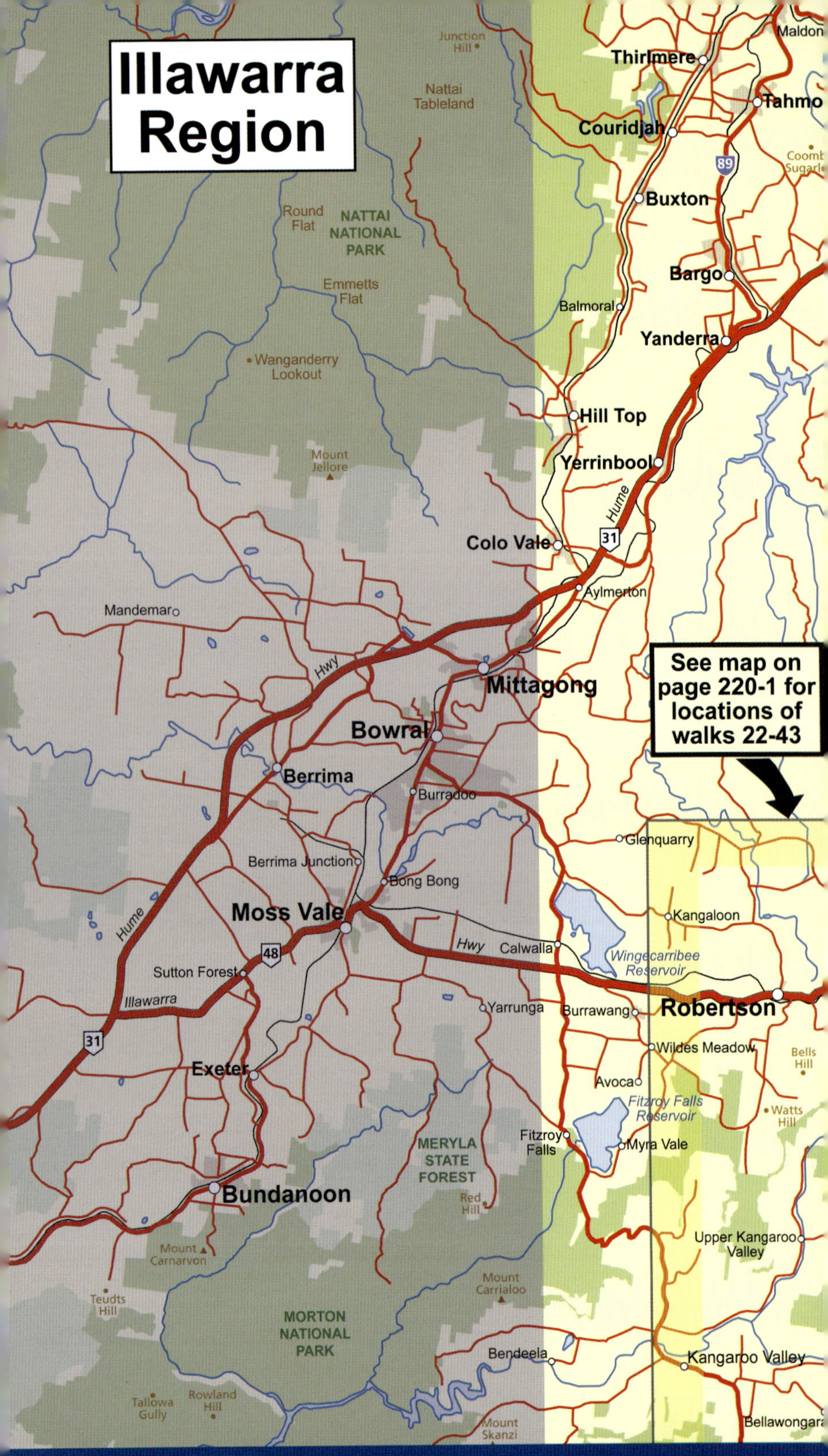

Illawarra Region
Junction Hill
Nattai Tableland
Round Flat
NATTAI NATIONAL PARK
Emmetts Flat
Wanganderry Lookout
Mount Jellore
Maldon
Thirlmere
Tahmo
Couridjah
Coomb Sugarl
Buxton
Bargo
Balmoral
Yanderra
Hill Top
Yerrinbool
Hume
31
89
Colo Vale
Aylmerton
Mandemar
Hwy
Mittagong
Bowral
Berrima
Burradoo
See map on page 220-1 for locations of walks 22-43
Glenquarry
Berrima Junction
Bong Bong
Kangaloon
Moss Vale
Hume
Hwy
Calwalla
Wingecarribee Reservoir
48
Sutton Forest
Illawarra
Robertson
Yarrunga
Burrawang
31
Wildes Meadow
Bells Hill
Exeter
Avoca
Fitzroy Falls Reservoir
Watts Hill
Fitzroy Falls
Myra Vale
MERYLA STATE FOREST
Bundanoon
Red Hill
Upper Kangaroo Valley
Mount Carnarvon
Mount Carrialoo
Teudts Hill
MORTON NATIONAL PARK
Bendeela
Kangaroo Valley
Tallowa Gully
Rowland Hill
Mount Skanzi
Bellawongara

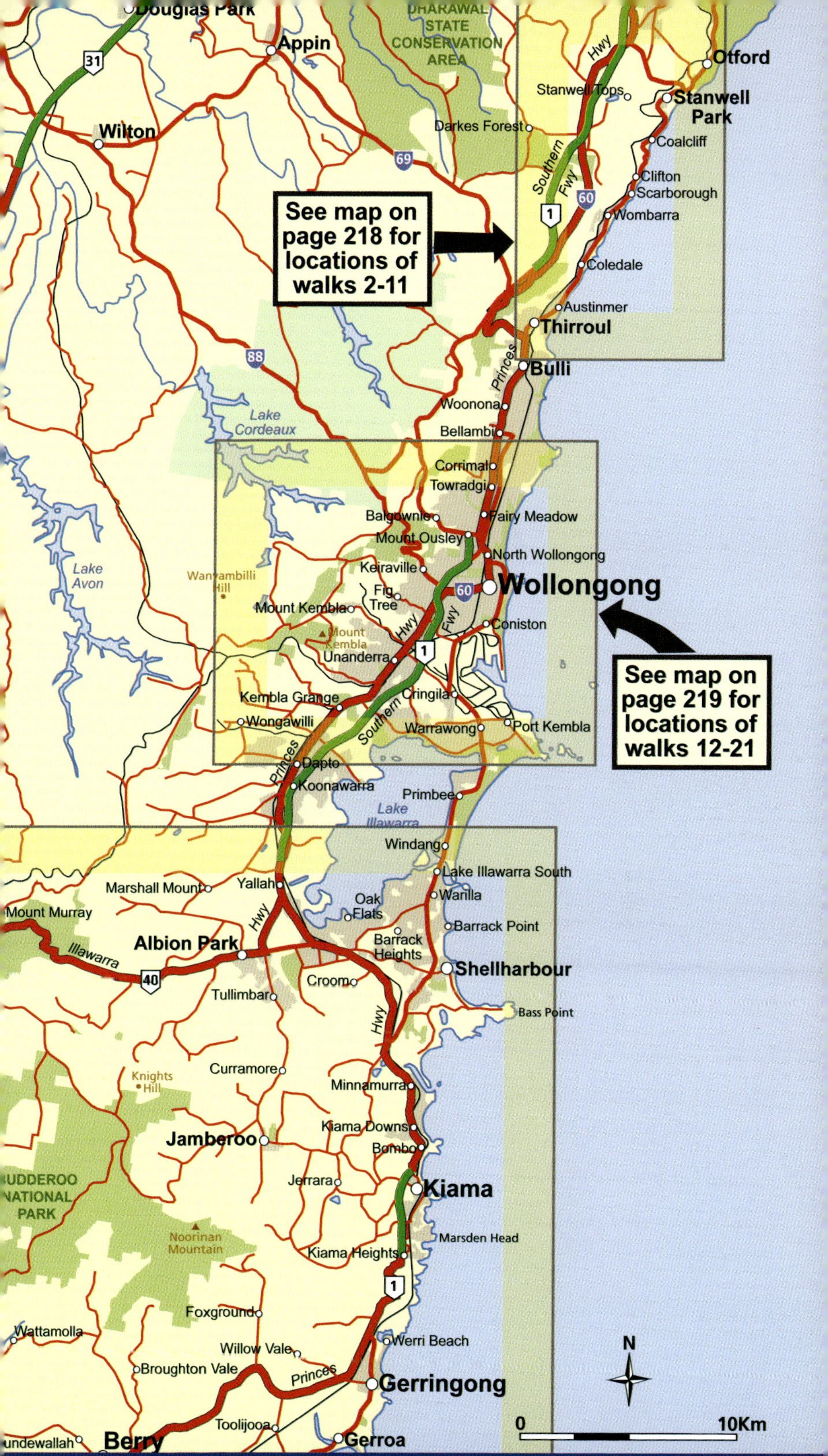
Douglas Park
Appin
DHARAWAL STATE CONSERVATION AREA
Otford
Stanwell Tops
Stanwell Park
Wilton
Darkes Forest
Coalcliff
Clifton
Scarborough
Wombarra
Southern Fwy
Hwy
See map on page 218 for locations of walks 2-11
Coledale
Austinmer
Thirroul
Bulli
Princes
Woonona
Bellambi
Lake Cordeaux
Corrimal
Towradgi
Balgownie
Fairy Meadow
Mount Ousley
North Wollongong
Keiraville
Lake Avon
Wanyambilli Hill
Fig Tree
Wollongong
Mount Kembla
Coniston
Unanderra
See map on page 219 for locations of walks 12-21
Kembla Grange
Cringila
Wongawilli
Warrawong
Port Kembla
Dapto
Koonawarra
Primbee
Lake Illawarra
Windang
Lake Illawarra South
Marshall Mount
Yallah
Warilla
Mount Murray
Oak Flats
Barrack Point
Albion Park
Barrack Heights
Illawarra
Shellharbour
Croom
Tullimbar
Bass Point
Curramore
Knights Hill
Minnamurra
Kiama Downs
Jamberoo
Bombo
Jerrara
Kiama
BUDDEROO NATIONAL PARK
Marsden Head
Noorinan Mountain
Kiama Heights
Foxground
Wattamolla
Werri Beach
Willow Vale
Broughton Vale
Gerringong
N
0
10Km
Toolijooa
Bundewallah
Berry
Gerroa
31
69
88
60
1
40

Contents

Introduction

The Illawarra is a special stretch of the New South Wales south coast, with a diversity of seascapes and mountain landscapes. Its name referred, for the Wodi Wodi people, to the district from where the Five Islands can be seen. Today we understand it to cover the land from Helensburgh to Gerroa, and from the coastal strip inland to the near highlands. The area's natural riches drew settlers to the Illawarra early: timber-getters, pastoralists and then miners. Despite the increasing population, there remains a wealth of walking here for those who know where to find it.

Fascinating underlying landforms – the Illawarra Escarpment and its outlying summits, volcanic flows and intrusions, sea-deposited dunes – have all created environments for a variety of vegetation. On foot, you can discover lagoons fringed with rushes, foothills draped in rainforest and – on top of the escarpment – heaths that bursts into flower in spring and early summer. There is plenty of other life too: the shoreline hosts intertidal creatures while lizards, wallabies and echidnas can be seen inland. The Illawarra is especially rich in birdlife, with visits from migratory waterbirds and plenty of permanent residents in forest and heath. Keep your eyes open, don't make too much noise and you'll discover a whole other Illawarra out there!

Kiama Coast Walk

Introduction

Walk grades and times

Each walk includes a grade, estimated time, distance and, where useful, total ascent and descent. The grade and estimated time probably err on the side of caution, but you'll soon figure out whether your own pace is faster or slower than that given and be able to make allowances. On occasion, times given in this book may differ from those on official signboards. If a walk is a half-day or less, no time has been allowed for a lunch break. The grade mainly reflects the terrain and the nature of the path, with consideration given to distance and ascent/descent. An **Easy** walk is likely to feature relatively level walking on a well-formed path (or along a beach) with only a few steps. Expect more steps or uneven surfaces in a **Medium** walk, perhaps with a less distinct trail to follow. A **Hard** walk requires good route-reading skill and includes rough ground and some very steep sections.

What to take with you

It is important to carry plenty of water with you, especially in warmer weather. In remote areas, be sure to take enough water for the whole walk, as creeks can run dry or be undrinkable if there is grazing or human activity upstream. Wear sensible shoes that have good grip and ankle support. Wear a hat, sunscreen and sunglasses. In cooler weather, make sure you have clothing that will keep you dry and therefore warm. Take some food with you, even for a short walk; eating something helps prevent fatigue and gives you an excuse for a rest. Keep a small, basic first-aid kit in the bottom of your day-pack.

Walking wisely

The Illawarra is blessed with a mild climate, especially near the coast. Walking in summer, however, can lead to heat exhaustion so on hot days restrict your walking to where there will be a coastal breeze or plenty of shade. If there is a risk of bushfire and during total fire bans, avoid walking in remote bush. In winter, the weather can be very changeable on the escarpment and you should take adequate clothing to keep you warm and dry. Spring and autumn are generally ideal for any walks.

Knowing your route

There are limited signed and waymarked walking tracks in the region so this book also makes use of other routes such as fire trails, unmapped tracks and intertidal rock platforms around headlands. On such 'unofficial' walks, it is especially important that you read the directions carefully, pay attention at junctions and check tide times where relevant. For most of the walks, the maps and directions provided in this book should be adequate for navigation. For a handful of the harder walks, however, you might carry the relevant topographic map with a 1:25,000 scale. Armed with this (and the skill to interpret it and use a compass) you'll be a lot safer if you lose the path. Of course, having a detailed map can add interest to almost any walk as you can identify landmarks from viewpoints and better understand the general lie of the land. There's no point carrying a GPS unit unless you know how to use it. Satellite (as well as mobile phone) signals may be limited in steep valleys or under thick tree cover.

Looking after the environment

It makes sense to preserve what attracted you to go walking in the first place, so here are some basic guidelines for walkers. If you're on a path, stay on it: taking shortcuts can cause erosion and damage vegetation. Pack a plastic bag for carrying out rubbish. If there are no toilets, bury human waste at least 15 cm deep and at least 100 metres away from any watercourse or track. Appreciate any native wildlife but don't get too close or you'll prevent it from feeding; don't offer it food yourself. Leave wildflowers and anything you find in rockpools undisturbed; likewise, leave fossils where you find them for others to enjoy. Observe any fire restrictions that apply and be very careful not to start any fires in the bush.

Safety tips

Several of the walks involve crossing rock platforms. Consult a tide chart and make sure you know what the tide is doing. Stay away in rough seas and big swells and never turn your back on the sea: every so often, a wave of increased size will sweep ashore. Take great care, too, near cliff edges and below cliffs as they can often be unstable. Ticks and leeches, although unpleasant, are rarely a serious threat to health. If you see a snake, stand still or stamp your feet; snakes nearly always move away when they feel the vibration of footsteps. Certainly, don't provoke it. In the very unlikely event that you're bitten, stay calm. Place a folded pad over the bite and apply a firm bandage over the pad and as far up the limb towards the heart as you can, splinting the limb with a stick to keep it immobile. You should remain still; telephone or send someone for medical help or wait for a passer-by to do so. Snakes are a good reason why walking solo is unwise.

Walking with children

Many of the shorter walks are suitable for children, but only parents can judge whether the distance and grade are suitable for their child. Toddlers may be carried in a purpose-designed backpack. The key to walking safely with children is supervision and a sensible ratio of adults to children. Extra care is needed on walks that feature unfenced lookouts or cliffs.

Taking your dog

No national park admits dogs and many regional parks and beaches also have restrictions. However, the 'Walks at a glance' summary lists several walks where you are welcome to take canine company, though note that almost all of these require that your dog be leashed.

Access to walks

There are various public transport options in this region. The South Coast rail line runs from Sydney off the escarpment to Stanwell Park and continues down the coastal plain through Wollongong to Kiama; change train here to continue south, as far as Bomaderry in the Shoalhaven. Bus services in the north are provided by Green's Northern Coaches and elsewhere by Premier Illawarra; see the back of the book for contact details to check current timetables. To access some of the walks, you'll require a car. A second car could prove useful for car shuffling for greater flexibility on a few walks.

Walks at a glance

	Walk	Page	Distance (km)	Time	Grade
Northern Illawarra					
1	Deer Pool & Marley Beaches	12	11.5 circuit	3 - 4 hrs	Medium
2	Burning Palms figure-of-eight	18	10.7 circuit	4 - 5 hrs	Hard
3	Maddens Falls	24	1.5 return	45 mins	Easy
4	Princess Marina Walk	28	2.5 circuit	1 hr	Easy
5	Stanwell Park scramble	32	5.5 loop	2 hrs 30 mins	Medium/hard
6	Wodi Wodi Track	38	7.7 circuit	3 hrs	Medium
7	Escarpment lookouts	42	5 return	2 hrs	Easy
8	Gibson Track & Sublime Point	46	3.5 loop	2 hrs 30 mins	Medium
9	Illawarra Escarpment traverse	50	18.5 one-way	7 - 8 hrs	Hard
10	Coalcliff to Scarborough	56	5.5 one-way	2 hrs	Easy
11	Wombarra to Thirroul	60	8 one-way	3 hrs	Easy/medium
Around Wollongong					
12	Bellambi Lagoon	66	7 circuit	2 hrs 30 mins	Easy
13	Brokers Nose / Corrimal	72	12.5 loop	4 hrs	Medium/hard
14	Wollongong's history	76	5 loop	2 - 3 hrs	Easy
15	Botanic Gardens & University	82	3.3 circuit	2 hrs	Easy
16	Mt Keira: sea to summit	86	4 one-way	3 hrs	Medium/hard
17	Mt Keira Ring Track	92	5.7 circuit	3 hrs	Medium
18	Summiting Mt Kembla	96	3.4 return	1 hr 45 mins	Medium
19	Circling Mt Kembla	100	5.5 circuit	2 hrs	Easy/medium
20	Port Kembla heritage	104	5.7 return	3 hrs	Easy/medium
21	Hooka Point	108	4.6 return	1hr 30 mins	Easy

Café	Dogs	Conditions	Highlights
-	-	Little shade	Waterhole, rock formations
-	-	Tide affected	Remote beach, rockpools
-	-	All seasons	Heath wildflowers, waterfall
-	-	Best after rain	Waterfalls, pre-war charm
yes	-	Exposed traverse	Wild coastline
-	-	Rough terrain	Cascades, viaduct, views, forest
yes	-	Best in Spring	Coastal views, wildflowers, birdlife
-	-	Steps; ladders	Rainforest, ladders, coastal views
-	-	Ill-defined track	Varied forest, sweeping views
yes	yes	All seasons	Sea Cliff Bridge, views, beaches
yes	yes	Tide options	Rock platforms, beaches
yes	yes	Best at low tide	Rockpools, coastal wetlands
-	-	Muddy after rain	Forest, heath, escarpment views
yes	yes	All seasons	Local history, coastal scenery
yes	-	Best in spring	Botanic diversity, birdlife, views
yes	-	Short scramble	Sculptures, forest, panorama
-	-	Steep and eroded	Rainforest, escarpment views
-	-	Includes scramble	Forest, wildflowers, views
-	-	Slippery after rain	Rainforest, mining history
-	yes	Best at low tide	Coastal scenery & platforms, history
-	yes	All seasons	Public art, birdlife, kids can cycle

Walks at a glance

Walk	Page	Distance (km)	Time	Grade
Around Shellharbour				
22 Lake Illawarra Entrance	114	6.5 one-way	2 hrs 30 mins	Easy
23 Shellharbour village	118	5.5 circuit	2 hrs	Easy
24 Bass Point Reserve	122	5 circuit	3 hrs	Medium
25 Minnamurra Spit & Killalea	128	11.5 circuit	4 hr 30 mins	Medium/hard
26 Macquarie Pass Cascade	134	2 return	1 hr	Easy
27 Waterfalls of Macquarie Rivulet	138	7 return	2 hrs 30 mins	Easy/medium
Jamberoo and above				
28 Jamberoo village	144	5.5 circuit	2 hrs 30 mins	Easy
29 Minnamurra Rainforest	150	4.2 circuit	1 hr 45 mins	Medium
30 Illawarra Lookout	155	2 return	1 hr	Easy
31 Griffiths Trail	158	8 circuit	3 hrs	Medium
32 Carrington Falls: south rim	162	5.5 return	2 hrs	Easy
33 Nellies Glen & north rim	166	5 return	2 hrs	Easy/medium
34 Belmore Falls	171	1 circuit	30 mins	Easy
35 Hindmarsh Ridge	174	12.5 return	4 hrs 30 mins	Medium
Around Kiama				
36 Kiama: a walk back in time	180	3.5 circuit	2 hrs	Easy
37 Spring Creek	185	3 one-way	1 hr	Easy
38 Minnamurra to Kiama	189	11 one-way	4 hrs	Easy/medium
39 Kiama to Gerringong	195	17 one-way	5-6 hrs	Medium
40 Bonaira Garden circuit	200	5.5 circuit	2 hrs	Easy
41 Hoddles Track & Saddleback	204	9.5 return	3-4 hrs	Medium
42 A Gerringong stroll	208	3.7 circuit	2 hrs	Easy
43 Black Head & Gerroa	212	8.3 return	3 hrs	Easy/medium

Café	Dogs	Conditions	Highlights
yes	-	Tide affected	Lake, rocky island, birdwatching
yes	yes	All seasons	Shore platforms, beach, local history
-	-	Rock-hopping	Aquatic reserve, history, wild coast
-	-	Easy option	River, coast & lagoon, birdwatching
-	-	Not in wet	Rainforest, cascade
-	-	Not in wet	Forest, escarpment views, waterfalls
yes	yes	Short option	Local history, rolling farmland
yes	-	Easy option	Rainforest, waterfalls
-	-	Best in spring	Wildflowers, view to coast
-	-	Best in spring	Heath, forest, birdwatching
-	-	Best after rain	Waterfall, wildflowers, views
-	-	All seasons	Cascade, forest, gorge views
-	-	Best after rain	Waterfalls, valley views
-	-	Avoid hot days	Forest trails, valley views
yes	yes	All seasons	Architecture, The Blowhole, views
yes	-	All seasons	Wetlands, birdlife, views
yes		Tide options	Rugged coast, volcanic formations
yes	-	No shade	Coastal downs, whale watching
yes	yes	All seasons	Beaches, garden, Little Blowhole
-	-	Steep in places	Farmland, escarpment, views
yes	yes	Tide affected	History, geology, whale watching
yes	yes	Tide affected	Shore life & geology, coastal views

Sea Cliff Bridge

The Northern Illawarra

To the north of Wollongong, the Illawarra Escarpment – the sharp edge of a sloping sandstone plateau – stands as a high wall, backing a strip of coastal plain with a succession of stunning beaches, each with its own sea pool. Coal measures below the sandstone were spotted by shipwreck survivors as they walked through the area in 1797 and today's quaint perched villages are a reminder of a mining heritage. Royal National Park, with its magnificent sweep of heathland and sea cliffs, is easily accessible from these northern villages and there are lots of other options here, with easy walking on the tops or along the beaches, or more difficult treks traversing the foothills of the escarpment or breaching the scarp and climbing to the plateau.

The South Coast rail line runs from Sydney, through the villages and continues south. Green's #2 bus (T 4267 3884, www.greensnortherncoaches.com.au) plies the road from Stanwell Park to Wollongong.

Coalcliff

1 Deer Pool and Marley Beaches

Wattamolla is a popular spot within Royal National Park and has a huge car park to prove it. Once you've found your way out of this, it is well worth diverting down to the beautiful beach and lagoon before (or after) the walk. You are more likely to find yourselves alone, though, at Deer Pool, mid-way along this walk, which also takes in dramatic cliff views, remote beaches and wild moors. Be warned that water from the tap near the Wattamolla kiosk is signed as not drinkable. You might collect safe drinking water from Wattamolla Creek, not long into the walk.

At a glance

Grade: Medium

Time: 3-4 hrs

Distance: 11.5 km circuit

Conditions: Little shade; avoid in hot weather

Getting there:

Car: From Sir Bertram Stevens Drive in Royal National Park, turn east into Wattamolla Road; car park at end

Walk directions

1 At the northern edge of the picnic area, not far from a kiosk and an information board, you'll find the Coast Track, signed to *Marley Beach*. Follow this to soon ford Coote Creek on rocks well behind the waterfall that plunges into Wattamolla lagoon. Detour out to the cliff edge (where there's a safety fence) for views over the lagoon. Returning to the track, climb some steps through heath to soon cross Wattamolla Creek just behind a low dam wall. Swimming is possible in the pool and it is worth clambering below the wall for views down the creek gully.

2 The path now climbs quite steeply up through a cluster of shapely boulders. Ascend more stone steps before the path, now eroded, levels out. Behind you the views open up with rolling, forested ridges and hills and the sea beyond.

3 When you reach a Y-junction, bear left down the path signposted *Little Marley Fire Trail*. This link track, after a kilometre, reaches an unsigned T-junction where you turn right onto Little Marley Trail. Along the broad, stony track are tea-tree, honeyflower (or mountain devil) and dwarf apple, a type of angophora. As you descend gently, more dramatic views open up of the sea cliffs north of Marley Beach.

4 At a marker post at a T-junction, a small sign points you left (north)

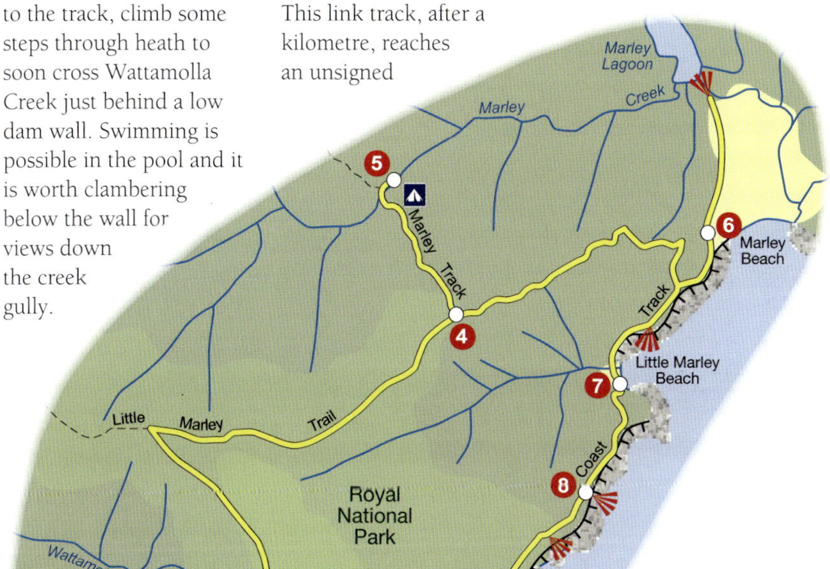

to Deer Pool on the Marley Track. This path soon braids - take the left, older looking branch which becomes narrow and a little overgrown, descending through sheltered forest to soon reach a bush-camp clearing (permit required). Soon after, the path crosses Marley Creek just above where it cascades down a broad rock shelf and empties into Deer Pool.

5 The pool is set prettily between fern-covered rock and a sandy beach: a great spot for lunch and a cooling dip. Retrace your steps along the Marley Track to the path junction (waypoint 4) and turn left downhill through tea-tree. The trail ends at a clearing where oleander

grows. The onward path is narrow and eroded, passing left of low rock outcrops to soon reach the junction with the Coast Track. Head left to reach Marley Beach.

6 This wild beach is never patrolled and rips make it a dangerous beach for swimming. Instead, it's worth crossing the extensive sand dunes behind the beach for views over freshwater Marley Lagoon, a haven for water birds and for introduced rusa deer alike. From Marley, retrace your steps a little way then continue southward on the Coast Track and, in about 600 metres, descend to Little Marley Beach.

7 Little Marley is a safer swimming beach and is backed by a miniature lagoon, edged by low open forest and grassy glades; there was once a youth hostel here. Cross the beach and ascend to the rocky cliff tops with dramatic views down to a rock platform. The path ascends on rock steps and follows along precipitous cliffs then leads up metal stairs and along a walkway.

8 You come to an exquisite cliff-top section of the path where the way is over eroded sandstone, tinctured and patterned with oxides. From here, there are stunning views in both directions. After hugging the dramatic cliff line for 1.25 kilometres, the path turns inland through heath and reaches the Y-junction (waypoint 3) where you turn left, retracing your steps to Wattamolla.

Out and about – The Coast Track

The classic walk of the Royal National Park is the Coast Track, which extends from Bundeena to Otford, leading you along the tops of sheer cliffs, over moorland, through rainforest and past secluded beaches. The track runs for 28 kilometres and can be completed in a long, strenuous-but-thrilling day. However, to allow time for swimming, to enjoy the magnificent coastal views, or simply for a more relaxed pace, you can break it up into two or even three days by camping (with a permit) or by staying overnight in the tiny youth hostel at Garie Beach. The route can be walked in either direction, although walking north to south keeps the sun behind you and offers a later transport link at Otford. Both ends are accessible by public transport; Otford is on the South Coast rail line and a ferry links Bundeena to Cronulla, which is on a branch line. The route, which is well waymarked, is described in detail in another book in this series, *Sydney's Best Bush, Park & City Walks*.

2 Burning Palms figure-of-eight

This walk makes good use of the Coast Track to enjoy a stunning section of Royal National Park coastline, taking you through high woodland with ocean views, down through rainforest to sand and surf. In addition, it visits a couple of the park's more secluded gems; if you don't like the idea of leaving the well-trodden way, you could detour to Werrong Beach on the official path and to the Figure of Eight pool via rock platforms from Burning Palms Beach.

At a glance

Grade: Hard

Time: 4-5 hrs

Distance: 10.7 km circuit

Conditions: Start shortly before low tide; some navigation off-track

Getting there:

Train: Otford station - cross rails via the bridge and climb steps to a fire trail; go left on Fanshawe Rd up to Lady Wakehurst Dr, then left for 200 m to Otford Lookout

Car: Otford Lookout is by a car lay-by on Lady Wakehurst Dr, about 2.5 km north of the junction with Lawrence Hargrave Dr

2 Burning Palms figure-of-eight

Walk directions

1 Before starting, take in the amazing views: northward spans most of the Royal's rugged coastline and to the south the escarpment extends to Port Kembla. Your way coincides with the classic *Coast Track* (which begins or finishes here), climbing north on steep log steps from the lookout. The track branches after 200 metres.

2 Continue ahead, following signs to Bundeena, ignoring the right fork signed to Werrong Beach (this will be the return track). This section of track, called the Cliff Track, climbs through tall forest of bloodwood and angophora onto Garawarra Ridge, becoming a more level fire trail.

3 About 20 minutes from the Werrong branch track, turn right at a T-junction signposted to *North Era and Garie Beach.* The track passes through tea-tree and heath and, in 500 metres, reaches the first of two short diversions (right) to rock ledges. The second provides a panoramic view south over Werrong Beach to Wollongong. Back on track, descend and soon cross a rill to pass a beautiful angophora, its roots splayed over an anchoring rock. After several minutes' descent on stone and log steps, a totem post is reached where the track swings left.

4 Remember this spot for your return. The main track now descends through littoral rainforest before levelling somewhat at the start of Palm Jungle. Apart from the tall cabbage tree palms, there are fig vines hanging from the canopy, tree ferns, birds nest ferns, elkhorns, coachwoods, and other rainforest species; it's a delightful place. After a kilometre or so in the rainforest, you'll reach a small grassy clearing on your right with signs of old campfires. Leave the path here and find, across the clearing, an eroded path descending steeply through lomandra to the right of an intermittent watercourse.

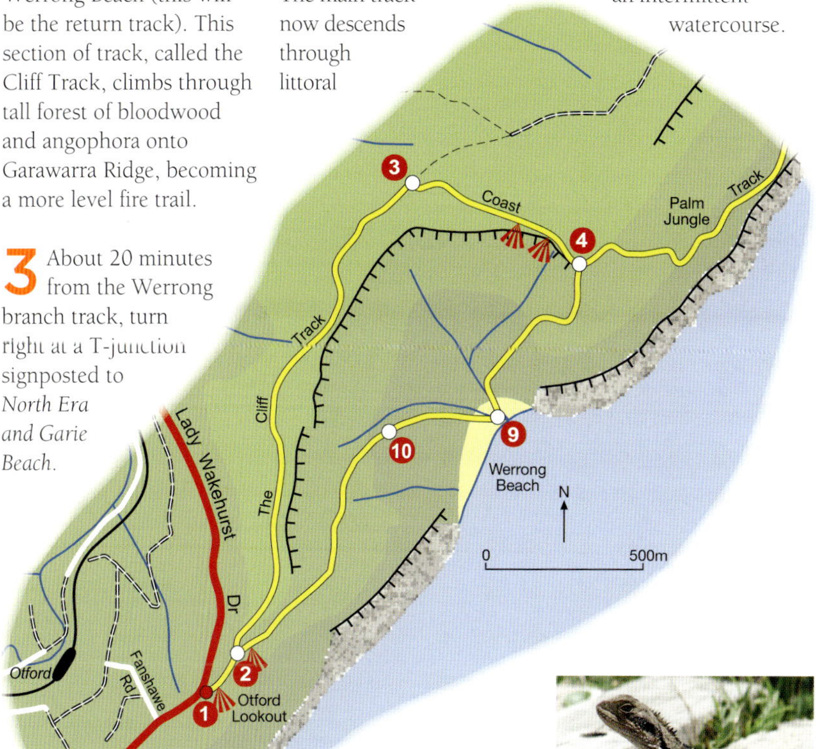

2 Burning Palms figure-of-eight

5 Aim for an obvious flat rock outcrop from where the rock platform below can be viewed. If the tide and swell are low (and the platform exposed) scramble down the gully where the scarp can be breached to reach the platform. Walk left under the cliffs for 100 metres to reach the Figure Eight Pool, just north of the point.

6 Here, two potholes formed by mineral and salt solution have coalesced in a perfect figure eight. The 3-metre-long pool is one of several near the water's edge; look for a footprint-shaped pool nearby. Now walk north around the headland on tessellated rock pavement, negotiating some large fallen rocks, to reach Burning Palms Beach.

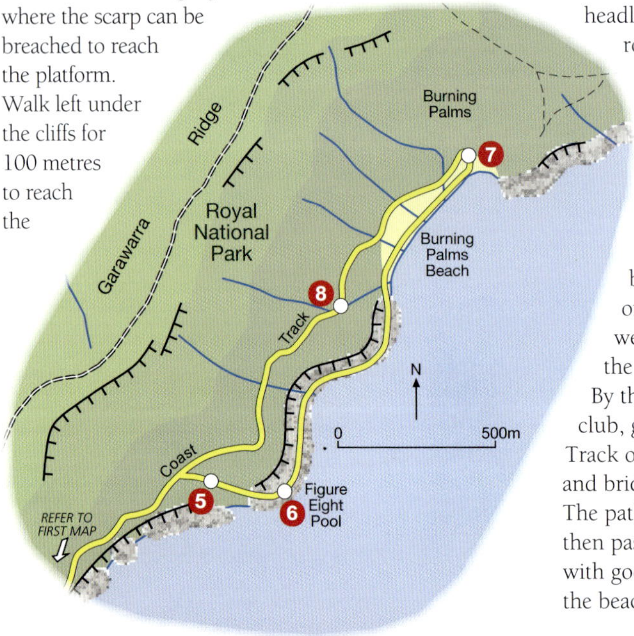

7 The northern end of the beach is patrolled on summer weekends so that's the place for a swim. By the surf lifesaving club, go left on the Coast Track on a metal walkway and bridge over Wren Rill. The path crosses more rills then passes a ranger's hut, with good views down to the beach.

8 The eroded path crosses more gullies before passing above the Figure Eight rock shelf and re-entering Palm Jungle. Return to the totem (waypoint 4) by a boulder mid-track. To reach Werrong Beach, make your way left on an indistinct path as it winds steeply downhill. After a while, the way is marked with faint yellow daubs and with ribbon. The footpad swings right and then steeply left (south). Track-finding becomes harder but you will be in earshot of the sea and should pick up the path again if you keep descending through the open under-storey. Reach the mossy boulders of an unnamed rill which can be followed to the northern end of Werrong Beach.

9 As you emerge, you may find you're the only people with clothes on: isolated Werrong is the only beach in the park allowing 'unclad bathing'. Have a good rest and admire the amphitheatre of cliffs to the north, before tackling the 200-metre haul back uphill. To reach the unsigned exit path, cross a second rill on stepping stones then follow the well-defined path that heads steeply up, above a deep creek gully through shady rainforest. The path veers left, passing right of a clearing fringed by cabbage tree palms.

10 Take a breather here before contouring the steep slope on an ascent to the ridgeline. The coastal views improve and then the path levels and joins the Cliff Track (waypoint 2). At the junction, detour left to a lookout rock for unimpeded views south, then continue downhill to the start point.

3 Maddens Falls

Much of the Woronora plateau - west of the Illawarra Escarpment - is off-limits, with large areas set aside for military activity, water catchment, or mining. This short walk in Dharawal State Conservation Area offers walkers a taste of the terrain and is worth lingering over as it leads through rare ironstone woodland and upland swamp to a charming waterfall. Further afield in the northwest Dharawal SCA (reached by car from Wedderburn Road) are the Jingga waterholes and a colony of koalas.

At a glance

Grade: Easy; variant is medium

Time: 45 mins

Distance: 1.5 km return

Conditions: Includes a short, steep section

Getting there:

Car: From Princes Hwy (not the Southern Freeway) turn west into Darkes Forest Road; after about 2.5 km, park in a lay-by on the left, by a NPWS info board

Walk directions

1 The signed track starts as a broad management trail that descends quite steeply. The forest here grows on a capping of ironstone, a chemical sedimentary rock that forms in swamps. Silvertop ash grows well here, sheltering geebungs, myrtles and wattles, with Gymea lilies scattered about. At the bottom is a junction - detour briefly left to view the upper reaches of Maddens Creek.

2 The dammed creek is broad here and the banks are a haven for many frog species, including the brown froglet, Perons tree frog and the delightfully named eastern pebblebonk. Return to the junction and follow a walk totem along steel mesh walkway that carries you over upland swamp. Fine organic material has accumulated above a layer of sandstone here and slowly releases moisture to a community of hardy plants such as hakeas, pink swamp heath, and sedges.

3 A brief detour left on a grassy track leads to an old picnic table by an old wall damming the creek. Back on the main path, the creek is out of sight as you walk parallel to it on more steel boardwalk to a lookout platform.

4 Maddens Falls cascade over a shelf of sandstone and the surrounding swamp ensures that it seldom runs dry. Below the sandstone shelf, more fertile soil supports a scrub of tea tree and native river rose under

coachwood and watergums. After enjoying the view, return by the same route.

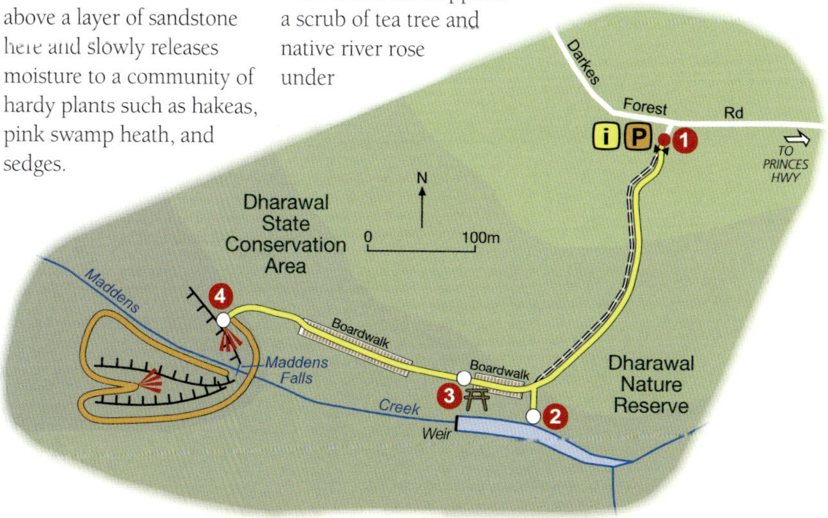

3 Maddens Falls

Walk variation

Competent scramblers can get a closer view of the falls from below on this more difficult extension. A few metres before the lookout enclosure, you can leave the boardwalk left and reach the stream bed above the falls. Cross the creek well back from the drop, with due care of slippery rock, and continue along the rock ledge beyond the falls. A relatively easy descent and a detour leads to a rock platform mid-level in the gully with a good view to the falls. Don't try to get down from here; follow the bench downstream some 100 metres before you reach a feasible way down. You can then boulder-hop and clamber over flood debris to the base of the falls, where ferns flourish in the moist, shady conditions. The easiest way back up is to return the same way.

Illawarra environment – The Gymea Lily

Any bushwalker who has read John Wyndham's *Day of the Triffids* will probably find the gigantic Gymea lily a little disturbing. *Doryanthes excelsa* is impressive enough in any season but when it sends up a tall spike that bursts into flower in spring and summer, it is downright astonishing. This giant was put to great use by Aboriginal people of the Illawarra: the flower was roasted and eaten, the stem served as a pole or a spear and the fibrous leaves could be turned into strong string. The early colonials took note and leaf samples were sent from Sydney to England to investigate whether a cord-making industry was viable. You'll likely see quite a few of these plants as you walk through their sclerophyll habitat. If they start moving towards you *en masse*, run!

4 Princess Marina Walk

Due to the lie of the land, few watercourses cascade over the sheer escarpment in the northern Illawarra. Luckily, at Stanwell Tops both Kellys and Gills Creek do and walkers can view both falls via the *Princess Marina Walk*. Developer Henry Halloran, who owned land from escarpment to ocean in the 1930s, had plans for a glamorous hotel and 'pleasure park' and built the path to what were then known as Romeo and Juliet Falls, now in the Garawarra State Conservation Area. The walk – named in honour of the visiting Duchess of Kent – was once a popular tourist attraction and still holds plenty of charm.

At a glance

Grade: Easy

Time: 1 hr

Distance: 2.5 km circuit

Getting there:

Train: From Stanwell Park station (1 km away), take the Wodi-Wodi path (see Walk 6) uphill and branch right to climb steeply; cross Hargraves Creek then go north on Stonehaven Dr

Car: Drive along Lawrence Hargrave Dr to Stanwell Tops; turn south into Stonehaven Dr and immediately park by the roadside

Walk directions

1 Walk through the tiny War Memorial Park and cross busy Lawrence Hargrave Drive, veering right to find a footpath near a tree signed *Princess Marina Cliff Walk*. The narrow path, which may be somewhat overgrown, is fairly level and leads through a forest of Sydney peppermints and broad-leaved Gymea lilies. Originally, linked tree branches formed a long avenue here. Descend slightly to pass Lovers Nook, overlooking a gully known as Undola Canyon. Note the heart decoration on the stone wall; Halloran was either a great romantic or a sharp marketer. Further along the path, you reach several stone steps up to a natural rock platform on the right.

2 Castle Rock boasts a battlement of mortared sandstone, but the effect is spoilt somewhat by modern safety fencing. There are views over twisted smooth-barked apples *(Angophora costata)* and Otford Valley. The main path descends gradually to cross a side creek on a plank bridge then ascends gently through an understorey of Gymea lilies and grass trees with a canopy of large scribbly gums and angophoras to another lookout, jutting into the trees. The gully narrows and the slope gets steeper. Pass a sandstone seating arrangement, in sight of the escarpment amphitheatre and in sound of the falls.

3 Further on, new steps lead off left while the old path continues, unfenced, above the gully. From it, you can detour to the base of the top cascades by scrambling down a slope, but take care near the edge as Kellys Creek drops 48 metres into the valley. Retrace your steps to the junction and go right up the steps to emerge at a car park. Take the onward track signed *Kellys Falls* to cross the creek above the cascades. The next old

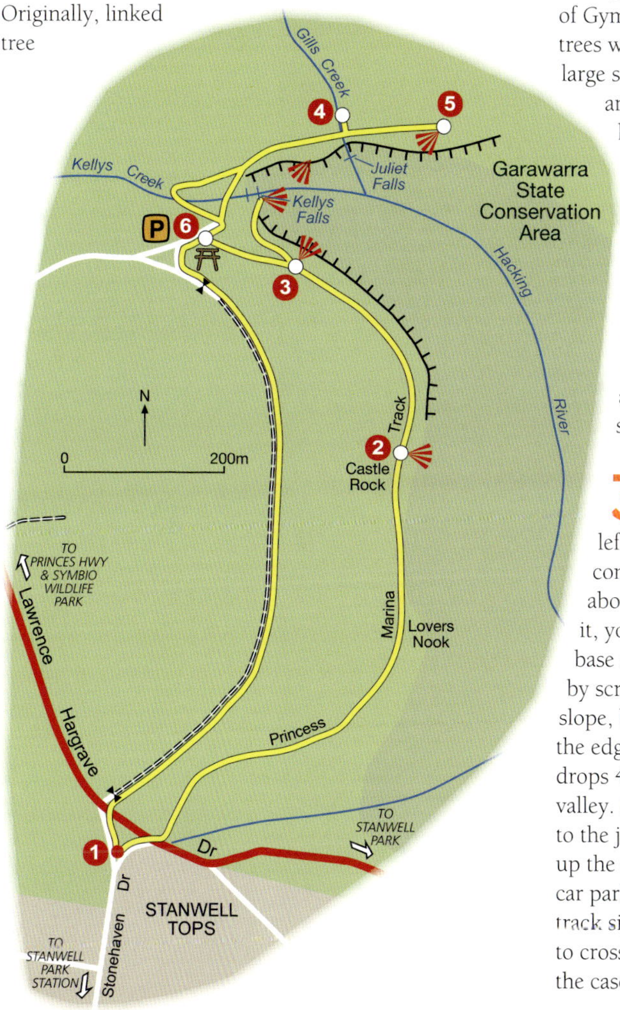

lookout may be overgrown but at the following one, where new railing keeps you back from the cliff edge, there are tree-filtered views. A short way on is Gills Creek.

4 Detour upstream on a footpad for a few metres to where the creek cascades by a stand of watergums; this shady dell is an ideal spot to linger. Return downstream and cross Gills Creek on stepping stones. The path brings you to another lookout known as Falls View, where the old walls are crenellated with red rock.

5 From here you can see the base of Juliet Falls and the whole of Kellys Falls (Romeo Falls in times of yore). For those wanting to extend their walk, a less defined path continues on along the escarpment from here, eventually joining a broader track that descends into the valley. Otherwise, retrace your steps over Gills Creek. By Kellys Creek, follow a path from the back of a cleared area that takes you 30 metres upstream and crosses the creek by the remains of an old wooden bridge, then back downstream to rejoin the main path and reach the car park.

6 From here you can return along the Princess Marina path or find a less interesting but more direct track that leaves from behind the furthermost picnic table; this exits, via a locked gate, onto Lawrence Hargrave Drive near the war memorial.

Out and about – Symbio Wildlife Park

There's plenty to catch the interest of kids on the Princess Marina Cliff Walk and it can be combined nicely with a visit to Symbio Wildlife Park, just nearby near the junction of Lawrence Hargrave Drive and Princes Highway. The park is spread over 16 acres of bush and parkland and has native, exotic and even farmyard animals, ranging from Tassie devils to rare monkeys and meerkats. There's even an opportunity to pat koalas and hand-feed kangaroos. Open 9.30 daily, www.symbiozoo.com.au, T 4294 1244.

5 Stanwell Park scramble

Just south of Royal National Park, Stanwell Park nestles in a sunny amphitheatre where the sheer Illawarra Escarpment temporarily recedes from the coast. Its idyllic beach is bookended by two small lagoons and backed by parkland where those brave enough to try hang-gliding aim to land. This short but adventurous walk takes you below their Bald Hill launchpad, beneath steep cliffs to an exquisite but hard-to-get-to rock platform. Stanwell Park Reserve has full amenities and a kiosk open daily.

At a glance

Grade: Medium/hard

Time: 2 hrs 30 mins

Distance: 5.5 km loop

Conditions: Avoid in heavy seas and high tide; path eroded and exposed in places; one assisted 3-metre clamber off rock ledge

Getting there:

Train: Stanwell Park station

Car: In Stanwell Park, leave Lawrence Hargrave Dr proper for the parallel local-traffic siding; turn off into Station St; car park in Stanwell Park Reserve

Walk directions

1 Walk through Stanwell Park Reserve to reach Stanwell Park Beach. The beach is patrolled seasonally so a swim could be in order. Walk over to the rocks at the beach's northern end; it's worth a short scramble to view two flat-topped pinnacles of rock standing on the point and to watch any surfers trying their luck.

2 Leave the beach on the northern side of Hargraves Creek inlet, usually closed to the sea. A narrow footpath ascends steeply to a car lay-by at a road bend on The Drive. Walk northeast along The Drive sharing, with the million-dollar houses, a grand coastal view to the south: beyond the famous Sea Cliff Bridge (see Walk 10) lie a string of northern Illawarra beaches.

3 As the road curves left (opposite number 87), continue ahead through grass and low scrub on an old vehicle track. You ascend steadily before the track levels and soon join a broader gravel trail, once part of the original railway.

4 Follow this right to reach a grilled tunnel entrance, emblazoned with graffiti. You'll find an easy way up the embankment to the right where an onward footpad follows above the tunnel entrance before diverging northeast and taking you through a forest of fig trees; the narrow but defined footpad is marked with mostly yellow daubs on trees and rocks. Presently the path descends then swings left to parallel high above the sea, contouring part-way up the steep hillside. The path is exposed in places so take great care.

5 When you reach a spur you'll find good views of the rock platform below.

Looking north, the sheer cliff line forms an arc, set back from the waterline in a rocky stretch known as Undola Beach. Descend the eroded path and make your way between and around large chunks of sandstone that long ago toppled from the cliff above: white paint daubs and the occasional arrow show the easiest route. Presently, the path descends to the rock platform to the left of an exposed

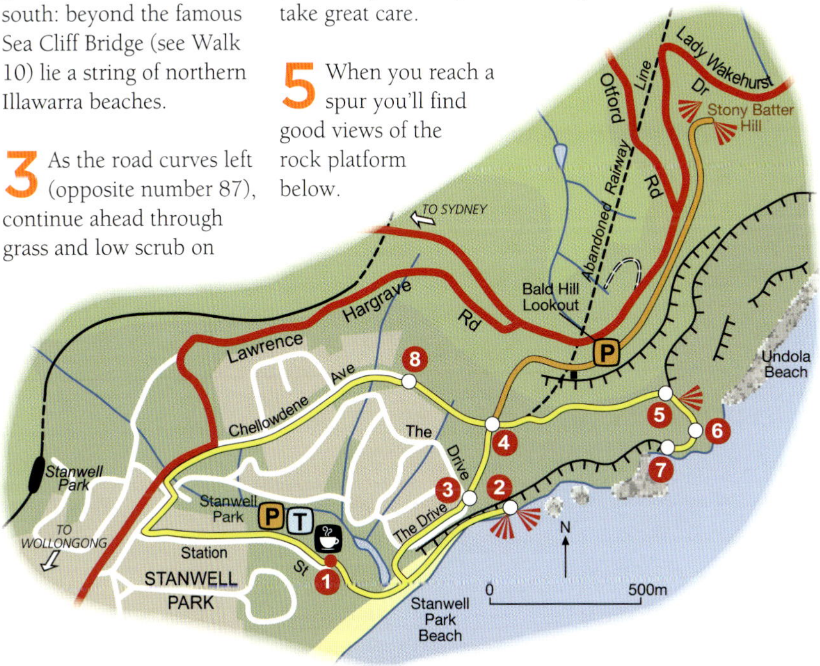

midden; remember this location for your return.

6 Heading south you'll reach a 'flow' of pale sandstone sitting atop a conglomerate base. Further along you must negotiate a 3-metre drop to a lower rock shelf. Steel spikes in the rock and a fisher's rope will assist the scramble but you shouldn't proceed unless you're confident you can get back up. Tide permitting, your objective is to reach a view of the same two rock pinnacles seen from waypoint 2, this time framing the dramatic scene of the coastline south.

7 Further progress south is barred by a

little cove where the rock platform gives way to a sheer rock wall, so you must return the same way. When you reach the old railway tunnel, continue along the gravel route of the former railway line until it joins Chellowdene Avenue.

8 Keep ahead here and turn left onto Lawrence Hargrave Drive for a return to Station Street via a handy take-away shop.

Walk variation

To extend the adventure you can take the steep and very direct route to Bald Hill Lookout and beyond. A narrow and overgrown footpad leaves from waypoint 4, opposite where you joined the former railway: look for coloured tape on shrubbery. The route climbs steadily and can be very slippery after rain. You emerge from moist forest onto a hillside of lomandra and soon reach the grassy slope below the Hargrave memorial and the Bald Hill car park where there's information about the art and science of hang-gliding and paragliding. The lookout is popular with sightseers, picnickers and bikers plying the winding coast road. Leave the crowds and walk up to the northern end of the lookout, picking up a level footpad to pass a cement tank. This footpad leads to the base of the ramparts of Stony Batter Hill; skirt left to find a get-up that allows scramblers to reach the hill's 260-metre summit near a white-topped post. A detour right, following yellow arrows past an old trig site, leads to rocky ledges over the sea; from one you can see both up and down the coast. Return the same way.

5 Stanwell Park scramble

Illawarra history – Hargrave and unpowered flight

Lawrence Hargrave was an Australian aviation pioneer who lived and experimented at Stanwell Park because of its excellent wind conditions. He was the quintessential nineteenth-century gentleman scientist and polymath: an explorer, mason, historian, astronomer and inventor. He invented the box kite and, on 12 November 1894 at Stanwell Park Beach, he successfully lifted himself 16 feet in a contraption consisting of four linked box kites and a slung seat. His box kites and his work on aerofoils and curved wing surfaces enabled the development of the first generation of European and American airplanes. Hargrave's working models came to be housed in a Munich museum and, ironically, most were destroyed by Allied aerial bombardment during World War II. He was long commemorated on the Australian $20 note and there's a memorial to him above Stanwell Park on Bald Hill, the most famous hang-gliding area in Australia.

The view from Bald Hill

6 Wodi Wodi Track

It's not often that you can start a scenic bushwalk circuit from a railway platform! The Wodi Wodi Track is named after the Aboriginal people who lived along the Illawarra coastline. It traverses the amphitheatre-valley of Stanwell Creek and takes you through varied environments: blackbutt forest, rainforest gullies, cliff base, escarpment plateau, beach, lagoon and village backstreets. There's even a short creek walk to get up close to an engineering landmark, an eight-arched railway viaduct.

At a glance

Grade: Medium

Time: 3 hrs

Distance: 7.7 km circuit

Ascent/descent: 400 m / 400 m

Conditions: Steep and eroded track in places

Getting there:

Train: Stanwell Park station

Car: Park near Stanwell Park station

Walk directions

1 Behind the station shelter on the western (northbound) platform of Stanwell Park rail station, a sign marks the track-head. Climb steeply, on steps at first, among Gymea lilies. A tall eucalypt canopy filters the view down to Stanwell Park village and beach. Pass an old stone seat to reach a junction with another arm of the Wodi Wodi Track.

2 The right fork (known informally as the Goat Track) climbs steeply to Stanwell Tops (a useful link to Walk 4 and Kellys Falls), but you should keep ahead downhill. The track rounds a steep rainforest gully before making a precipitous descent – at times rough and slippery – to ford Stanwell Creek.

3 Hidden along the moss-covered boulder bed of Stanwell Creek are many pools and cascades and upstream the creek plummets over the escarpment as Stanwell Falls (not shown on the map). For a frog's-eye view of the historic viaduct, detour 300 metres downstream: follow the right bank past a swimming hole, and a few minutes of rock-hopping brings you to a double cascade then, several minutes later, to the creek's bedrock beneath the viaduct.

4 The 65-metre-high rail viaduct spanning Stanwell Creek was built in 1920 when the dangerous rail line was rerouted. It is the tallest engineering feat of its kind in Australia and a very impressive sight so close up. Return to the fording place and climb steeply out of the creek gully through a copse of cabbage tree palms. The path drops steeply to cross a branch creek, with yellow metal arrows marking the way. Climb steeply out of this gully and swing right as a broader track soon merges from the left. There's more ascent through open blackbutt forest with filtered sea views before the path levels on a broad bench below the escarpment.

5 Two kilometres from the station you reach a signed junction, where you should detour right, uphill on the Bullock Track, an historic route used by early European settlers. Follow in their footsteps up an initially steep, stepped incline. The track levels somewhat to follow the base of the scarp – look out for original flagstones on this section – before swinging left to breach the cliff line. There are good

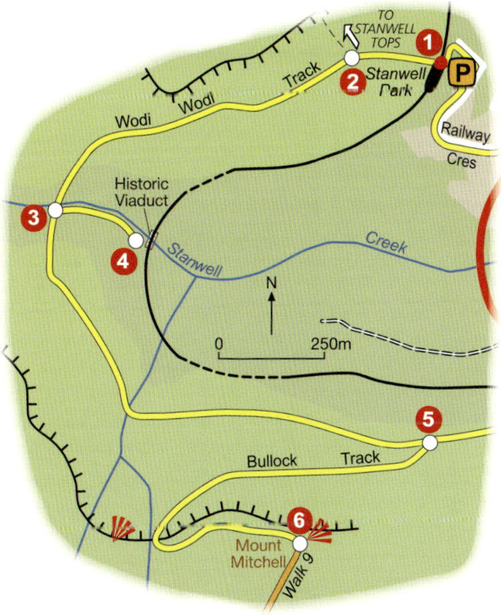

views from the nearby rock ledge, west of the track. Now follow the continuing path for a few hundred metres through angophoras and Gymea lilies.

6 When you reach a group of rocks on your left, you might take a well-earned rest on the north-facing bluff of Mount Mitchell. The views from this superb vantage point take in Stanwell Park, Bald Hill, Royal National Park and even the Sydney city skyline on a clear day. The Bullock Track, if continued on, links to the Forest Walk (see Walk 9) but you should now return to the junction at waypoint 5 and turn right, following the Wodi Wodi Track signed to *Coalcliff* station and descending through blackbutt forest on a broader track.

7 Emerge from the forest and walk down a grassy hill where there's a NPWS information board. Cross a boardwalk and pass left of a disused stile then below the railway tracks via a pedestrian tunnel. Head left, following beside a high wire fence to parallel both rail and road for 400 metres or so, looking north to see Bald Hill and Stony Batter Hill.

8 The path swings right and descends to cross Lawrence Hargrave Drive (the original route of the rail line) where you should look for a little metal sign with a walker icon for the narrow footpath down-slope to a three-way road junction: go ahead on Kallaroo Avenue which soon swings left steeply downhill to give walker-only access to Stanwell Park Beach.

9 Walk north on Stanwell Park Beach – *Dooundong* to the Wodi Wodi – crossing the shallow outlet of Stanwell Creek's lagoon (depending on flow, you may need to remove shoes here). The lagoon is a refuge for water birds and there's a chance to see swamp hens, dotterels, plovers, grebes, pipers and tattlers, among others. Continue past one of Australia's oldest surf lifesaving clubs: this is the place for a well-earned swim. Leave the beach just before its smaller northern lagoon to reach Stanwell Park Beach Reserve.

10 The reserve has full amenities and a welcome kiosk, open daily. From here, follow a signed footpath around the northern perimeter

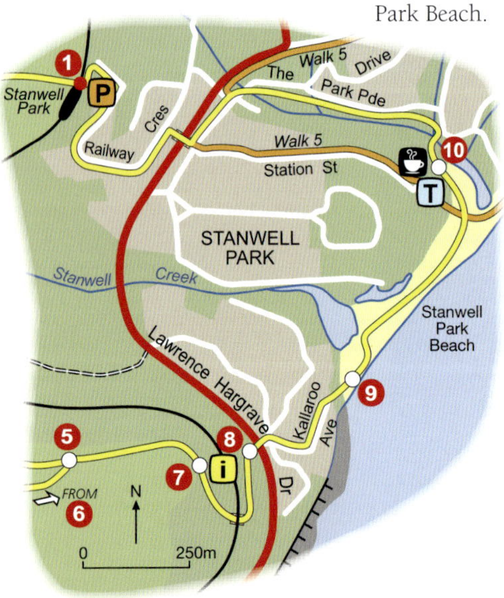

of the reserve. It takes you through a turpentine grove, across a footbridge over Hargraves Creek and joins The Drive. Go left here and left again at a parallel siding of Lawrence Hargrave Drive. Opposite Station Street, head right up steps and cross the footbridge over the main road. Turn left on Railway Crescent, winding uphill to return to Stanwell Park station.

Illawarra heritage – The Wodi Wodi

Aboriginal people have enjoyed what the Illawarra has to offer for over 30,000 years. Traditional stories of the Dharawal people tell of their arrival at the mouth of Lake Illawarra having come by canoe from the north, bringing with them the cabbage tree palm or *dharawal* which gives their language its name. This sacred rainforest tree had many uses: its fibres made a strong rope and served in brooms, the leaves could be woven into baskets and the heart was cooked and eaten. The Wodi Wodi – speaking a variant of the Dharawal language – developed various routes as they travelled inland or north-south; many are now present-day roads and walking paths.

7 Escarpment lookouts

Vehicles whizz down the Southern Freeway without giving passengers or drivers much chance to enjoy the view off the plateau's edge. They're not just missing a panorama over the coast; there's a strip of bush along the cliff tops that is home to a variety of wildflowers, birds and lizards, all of which can be appreciated far better on foot. Refreshments are on offer along this short, level walk, plus a visit to the Southern Gateway Centre, which – true to name – is inaccessible by car if you're heading north.

At a glance

Grade: Easy

Time: 2 hrs

Distance: 5 km return

Finding the track

Get onto the Princes Highway, off Mt Ousley Road if heading north or off the Southern Freeway if heading south. Follow signs for Sublime Point, turning east into Lady Fuller Park to reach Sublime Point car park in 300 metres.

Walk directions

1 Beyond NPWS information boards, the lookout from Sublime Point Trig offers a stunning view over the coastline. Directly below is Austinmer and its beach, then, looking south, the points of Bulli, Waniora, Bellambi, Flagstaff (with Wollongong's lighthouse) and Red Point at Port Kembla, with Big Island offshore. Head right on a concrete path and pass walk information and a path descending to Austinmer. Beyond this is a sign: *Bulli Lookout - Sublime Point link track*. Beside it, a path leads off amid bracken fern into woodland, very soon passing exposed rocks on the left.

2 About 350 metres from the start, an old metal arrow directs you left. The track descends, eroded and overgrown in places, and swerves around through heath to parallel the escarpment. The wildflowers along the path are varied, with white coral heath, hakea and flannel flowers (including the delicate 'lesser' version), golden bush-peas, bright red honeyflowers or mountain devils, and an interesting diversity of banksias; in a damp stretch, watch for carnivorous sundews underfoot. After a view of cliffs, the path passes under transmission lines and joins a broader gravel track inland, reaching the road at a barrier gate.

3 The onward route skirts left, on an old vehicular track, fringed with Gymea lilies in taller forest. After almost another kilometre of easy walking, exit suddenly from the scrub into the grounds of Panorama House.

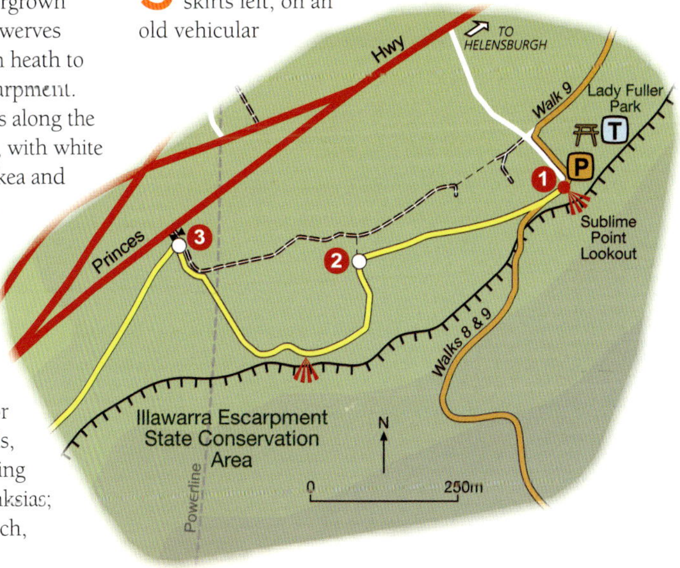

7 Escarpment lookouts

4 The best views are restricted for guests of the function centre, which is open for lunch. Cross the large car park and walk down a long avenue that leads to the gateway for Hopetoun Park. Steps up off the lane allow you to walk along the top of the cliffline, enjoying the view between trees.

5 The pleasant Cliffhanger café-restaurant is open daily and its terrace offers a superior view (especially with the coin-fed binoculars) over Bulli Point and Waniora Point. Looking southwest along the scarp, you can see another railed lookout and the Southern Gateway Centre beyond that. Walk through parkland to the lower lookout, which juts out on a sandstone ledge.

6 From this vantage point, you have a better view back along the escarpment to Sublime Point. The exposed beds of Hawkesbury sandstone have clear fault lines; when these weaken sufficiently, large blocks fall away. On top, the vegetation at the cliff edge has been shaped by strong winds. From here, retrace your steps to the start point.

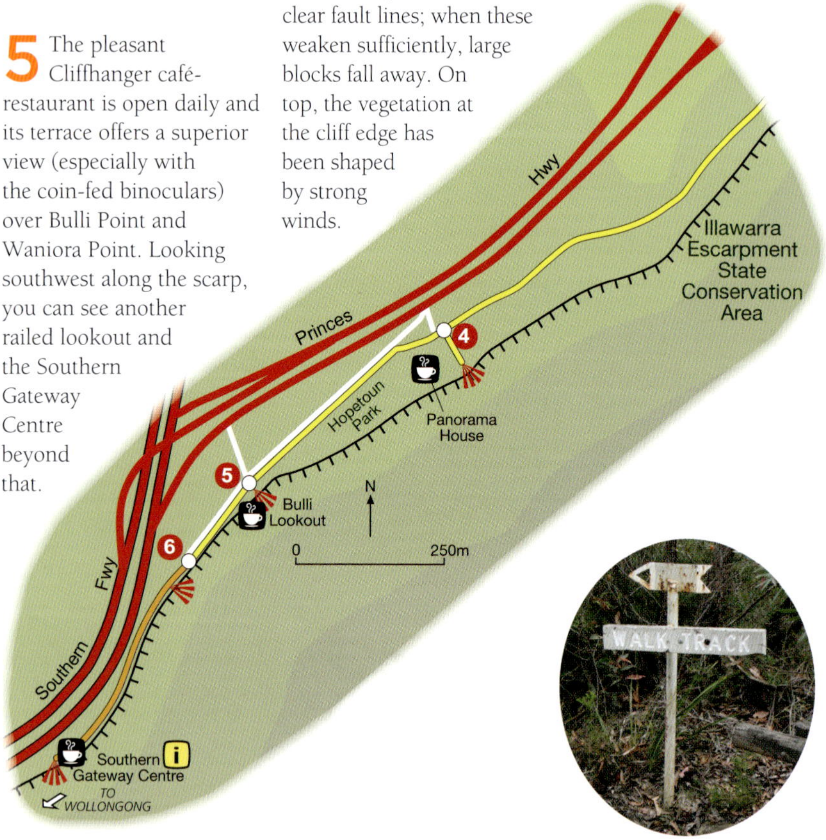

Walk variation

This walk could easily be linked with Walk 8, using the hardware at Sublime Point to get down off the escarpment. Even if you don't descend the whole way to Austinmer rail station, the lush vegetation that grows on the shale and claystone just below the cliff line is an interesting contrast to the heath and woodland on the tops, plus there's the sheer fun of clambering up and down metal ladders to be had!

Out and about - Southern Gateway Visitor Centre

Just half a kilometre further along the escarpment from the Cliffhanger is the flash Southern Gateway Visitor Centre, although you'll have to briefly skirt the busy freeway to reach it. As well as another lookout (where an orientation board puts a name to landmarks below), a café and visitor information service, the centre also houses the Jumbulla Aboriginal Discovery Centre, focusing on the social history and culture of the Aboriginal people of the Illawarra and South Coast. Jumbulla is open 0900-1700 daily; adult $15, child 5-16 years and concession $10.50, child under 5 free; www.jumbulla.com.au; T 4267 5894.

8 Gibson Track and Sublime Point

The Illawarra Ecarpment rises up from the coastal strip like a fortification and there are few points where it can be breached. It is possible at Sublime Point, however, with the aid of an elaborate series of steel ladders. This historic path dates back to 1916 when Sydney day-trippers would arrive by steam train and ascend old wood-and-steel ladders to take in the 'sublime' views. On the way up, walkers have a great opportunity to explore the upper bench of the escarpment, where eroded soil has built up on a shelf of more resistant sandstone to support rich vegetation. The panorama from the plateau is a fair reward for the effort you'll need to make!

At a glance

Grade: Medium

Time: 2 hrs 30 mins

Distance: 3.5 km loop

Ascent/descent: 290 m / 290 m (more from station)

Conditions: Includes ladders and many steps

Getting there:

Train: Austinmer station (1 km); from the overpass, walk up Hill St

Car: From Lawrence Hargrave Dr, turn into Moore St in Austinmer; cross the rail line by the station and keep left to climb Hill St; park at end of Foothills Rd

Walk directions

1 At the very end of Foothills Road, take the track signed *Phillip Street Fire Trail*, soon crossing over Flanagans Creek. At a junction, fork right and walk uphill on a track scattered with coal. Beyond the gate the track swings right to enter a clearing at the simple Austinmer Camp, set among tall blackbutts. Cross the clearing and, on its northeastern edge, pick up the Gibson Track, named in honour of a keen local naturalist.

2 Enter rainforest and pass the left-branching Bulli Lookout Track, now closed due to instability. Cross the creek once more and follow along the relatively flat bench, with gentle undulations. The rainforest – or closed forest, as it is also called – has a dense canopy of figs, scentless rosewood, impressive cabbage tree palms, and vines. A sudden clatter of wings probably means you have disturbed a wonga pigeon, feeding on the forest floor. The path passes right of a small swamp filled with rushes, set among red cedars and cabbage palms with a view up to the escarpment. After a section of boardwalk, you reach a junction.

3 Turn left here onto the Sublime Point Track, which climbs gently at first. An unsigned path joins in from the right and the slope becomes steeper. Steps up this section have recently been rebuilt and it is now much less slippery than it once was. After a stiff uphill stretch through tall turpentines and blackbutt, you reach the base of ladders, also recently improved at great cost by NPWS.

4 Make your way up the steel ladders and pause at the top to enjoy the view over the canopy. The climb is not over: a series of steep steps leads up through dense vegetation. Eventually, you emerge at Lady Fuller Park on the lip of the escarpment. Follow a path right to reach the Sublime Point trig and lookout. From here, you have a sweeping view over the coast, north over the coastal villages to Austinmer below, and

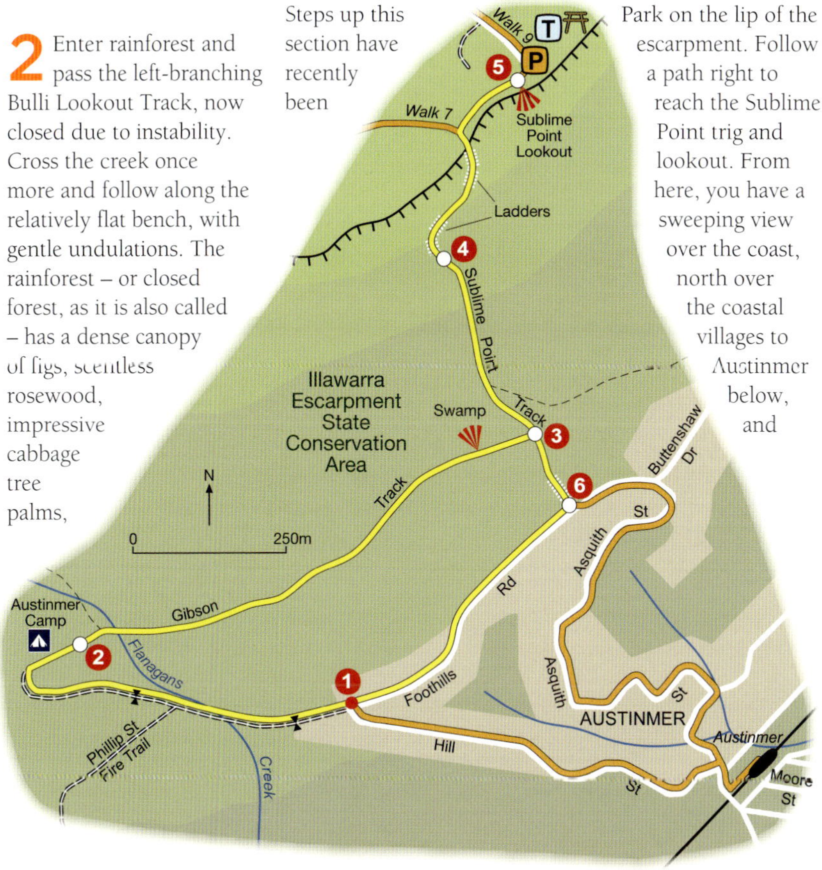

south over Bulli Point, Bellambi Point and the Wollongong headland to Red Point at Port Kembla and Big Island, the largest of the Five Islands.

5 After enjoying the panorama, descend the ladders and steps carefully. Ignore the unsigned junction and reach the junction at waypoint 3 where you continue straight ahead. The vegetation changes suddenly and you descend by a long series of steps off the face of the bench and exit the woodland on a right-of-way.

6 To return to your car, turn right and walk along Foothills Road; to return to the station, turn left and then keep right to follow Asquith Street as it winds downhill, then turn right into Balfour Road to soon regain the station.

Illawarra environment – bloodsuckers!

Leeches thrive in the moist environment of a rainforest and are especially active after wet weather. These carnivorous worms wait in low vegetation along paths for a warm-blooded animal to pass by, then attach themselves with incredible efficiency and make their way into your boot and through socks. While a tad unpleasant, leeches are not painful (they use a local anaesthetic) and the first sign most walkers notice is a bloodied sock, well after the walk is finished. The bite, however, is often itchy and can become infected. The ideal way to remove one is by applying salt or a lighted match, but most walkers just pull them off and perhaps dab on some antiseptic. To deter leeches, you might spray some insect repellant on your ankles and shoes. Staying still is an invitation for them to latch on, so watch where you sit or stand when hanging about.

9 Illawarra Escarpment traverse

This is the most challenging walk in the book, making for a big day out as you traverse the longest continuous stretch of the Illawarra Escarpment State Conservation Area. This has only recently been made feasible with the reopening of the historic Sublime Point Track and cutting of a new path that links the Forest Walk with the track system at Sublime Point. There's plenty to hold your interest, with a succession of stunning lookouts, a diverse range of plant communities and some delightful creeks and rainforest gullies.

At a glance

Grade: Hard

Time: 7 to 8 hrs

Distance: 18.5 km one-way

Conditions: See Walks 6 and 8; part of Forest Walk is ill-defined - track-finding ability needed

Getting there:

Train: Board at Austinmer station; alight at Stanwell Park station

Car: Park near Austinmer rail station and catch a train to Stanwell Park

Walk directions

1 From Stanwell Park station, follow the walk directions to the seventh waypoint of Walk 6, the Wodi Wodi Track. Time may not allow the creek-walk detour to the rail viaduct. The spectacular rock viewpoint on Mount Mitchell is an ideal stop for a snack and a rest where you can soak up the northern coastal views beyond Stanwell Park.

2 There's a sign describing the Forest Walk that you are now on. Continue southwest through woodland of bloodwood and twisted angophoras. You can keep detouring left from the track to the rock platform for views. Where the track veers right, an obvious footpad ahead diverts you to a view of the Sea Cliff Bridge south of Coalcliff and the coastline south to Port Kembla and beyond. The track – an old service trail – arrives at a water reservoir reached by a truck access road (the track traverses land owned by Kembla Coal and Coke).

3 The onward path can be hard to find: keep left of the fenced reservoir; there's a cleared track here but you should leave this left by a tree almost immediately onto an ill-defined footpad. The path improves but is at times narrow and overgrown, quite difficult to follow, especially when it traverses an exposed sandstone ridge top. Look for faint arrows on rock and sporadic interpretive signs.

4 When you emerge at a power-line service trail, go left briefly to reach two wooden posts, one on the left and one just after on the right of the trail. Head right at the second post, on an overgrown footpad, to enter some blackbutt forest. Cross another access road and

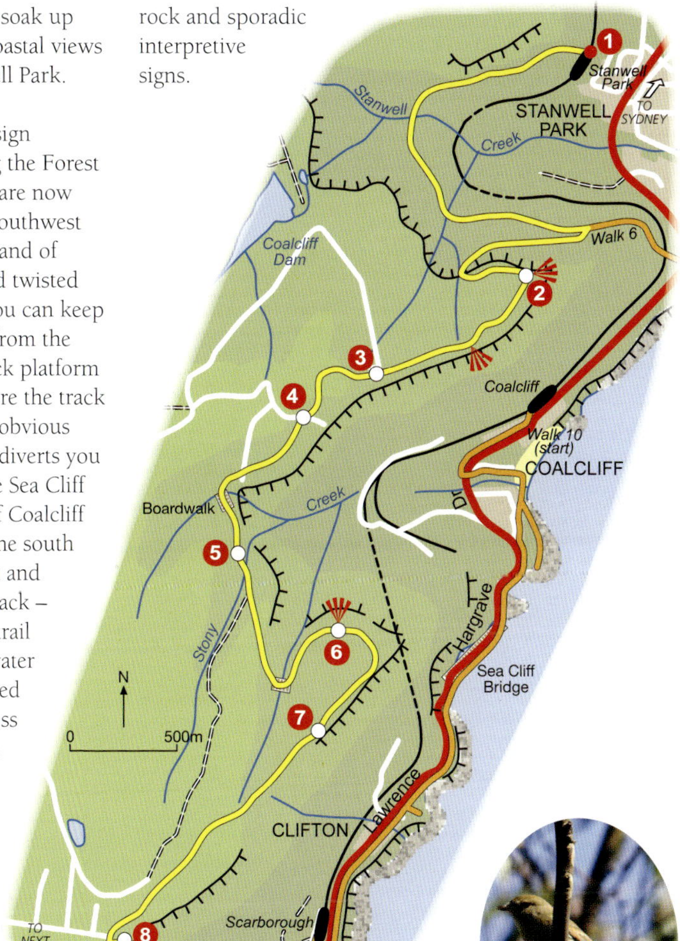

two minor streams, one on a dodgy footbridge. Soon you'll come to a boardwalk protecting fragile sedges growing on deep, moist alluvial soil. There's rich plant life here, including coral fern and coral heath, swamp banksias and native broom.

5 After crossing an arm of Stony Creek on bedrock, ascend and soon descend through grass trees, Sydney peppermints, angophoras and cabbage tree palms to a second, more deeply incised creek branch, crossed on a wooden bridge. You can rock-hop a short way downstream to view the water plummeting sideways over falls before doing a 90° turn. Just up from the creek, a broader trail merges from the right and there's a short detour left to the cliff line for an uninterrupted view over Coalcliff's colliery and harbour.

6 The path crosses another smaller creek and there follows the steepest climb of the Forest Walk out of a lyrebird gully. The air becomes noticeably cooler as the path edges close to the cliffs. You're now on a narrow ridge between a creek gully and the escarpment. Where the path drops down along the inner slope, grass trees, Gymea lilies and beard heath proliferate.

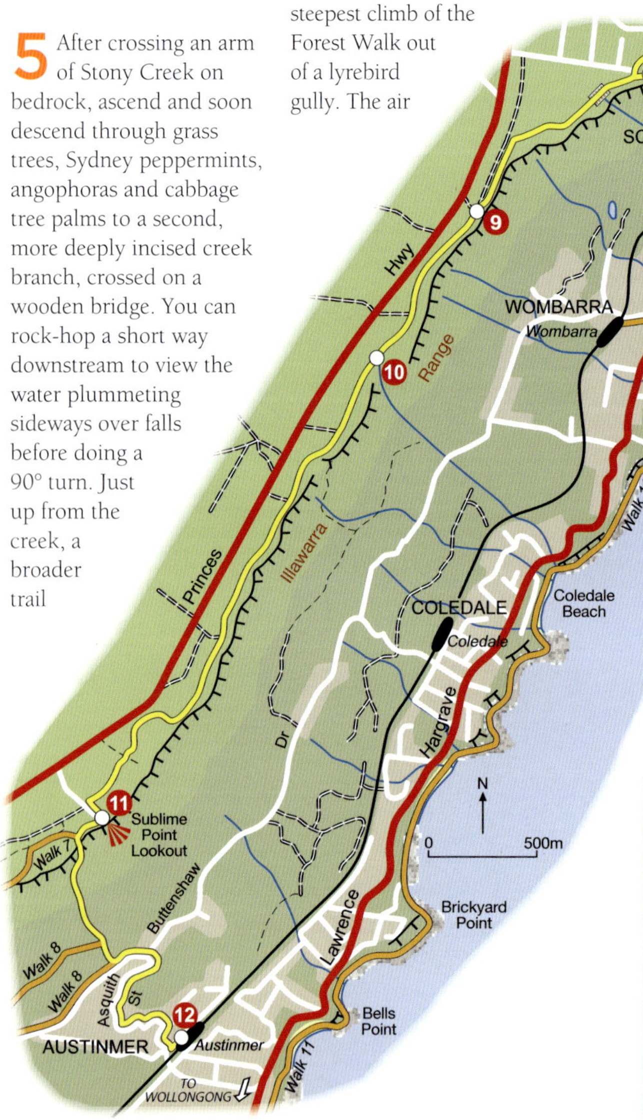

7 When you reach a signboard about the rainforest, detour briefly left through stunted, wind-sheared trees to a sheer cliff lookout for sweeping coastal views south. Back on the main trail, climb gradually through a protected ribbon of rainforest with lillypilly, coachwood, cabbage tree palms, corkwood and scentless rosewood. The Forest Walk ends without fanfare at another access road. A detour left to the road-end brings you to Trevorrow Trig.

8 NPWS have recently cut a path to link the Forest Path with Sublime Point. At the time of writing, there were not yet signs - in the absence of any, proceed as follows. Turn right onto the access road and pass

through a usually open gate then, immediately after, turn left into the forest on a footpad to soon cross a creek on a very new footbridge. When you reach a management track, turn left and follow this to three giant power poles at the end.

9 Take care as you enjoy the view from the cliffs overlooking Wombarra. A few metres back from the edge, pick up another footpad plunging you back into the forest. This threads its way along the narrow strip between the Princes Highway and the escarpment, through

Walk variation

If two cars are available, the walk could be shortened by leaving a car on the Princes Highway near the southern end of the Forest walk (4.3 kilometres north of the Sublime Point access road) or at Sublime Point car park.

bracken fern, Gymea lilies and an array of flowering plants including wedding bush. Continue on past several old access trails to your right.

10 The path drops down past a crop of rocks near the headwater of Stockyard Creek and then climbs gently out of the gully. The link track eventually brings you out onto the northern extremity of the Woodward Track loop. Head left, closer to the escarpment. The track's two railed escarpment lookouts have been closed due to unstable cliffs. After several hundred metres, you'll emerge at the Sublime Point car park and picnic grounds.

11 Past an information board and toilets are the railed lookouts of Sublime Point, one of the Illawarra's best coastal vantage points. From here, the views sweep from the northern Illawarra coastal villages south to Port Kembla and beyond. See the walk directions for Walk 8 to get from here to Austinmer station via ladders on the Sublime Point Track.

12 The steep road walk down to Austinmer rail station is hard on the calf muscles at the end of such a long day, so celebrations are in order.

Illawarra environment – Escarpment north to south

A long-distance walking track along the Illawara's iconic escarpment is a long-held dream that has inched closer to reality now that some small land parcels have been added to the estate managed by the NPWS. The concept of a continuous 250-kilometre track between Royal National Park in the north and Morton National Park in the Shoalhaven is an audacious one, but a shorter continuous walk between Bundeena and Mount Kembla – incorporating the popular Coast Walk and linking all the visitor facilities along the escarpment – could be achieved with minimal new track work. When it comes to long-distance walks, New South Wales has fallen behind Victoria and Queensland in recent years: just think of Victoria's *Great Ocean Walk* and Queensland's eight new *Great Walks*. A week-long walk of this quality so close to Sydney would go a long way towards redressing this imbalance.

10 Coalcliff to Scarborough

Steeped in mining history, Northern Illawarra's villages nestle against the Illawarra Escarpment along one of Australia's most spectacular stretches of coastline. This mostly roadside walk links picturesque Coalcliff and Scarborough with a walk over the iconic and aptly named Sea Cliff Bridge, the region's unusual tourist attraction. This walk connects easily with Walk 11, from Wombarra to Thirroul.

At a glance

Grade: Easy

Time: 2 hrs

Distance: 5.5 km one-way

Conditions: Take care on Coalcliff Beach's southern rock platform

Getting there:

Train: Start at Coalcliff station; finish at Scarborough station

Car: Park near Scarborough railway station and catch a train back to Coalcliff

Dogs: Allowed on leash

Walk directions

1 Leave Coalcliff station on the east side, down the steps, and turn right onto Lawrence Hargrave Drive. Turn next left on an unnamed lane leading downhill to Coalcliff Beach Reserve with access to the patrolled beach and the surf lifesaving clubhouse.

2 Coalcliff Beach is where the escarpment meets the sea, making for spectacular beach scenery. After taking in the cliff views, walk the beach south and over rocks by the sea-filled swimming pool. It's well worthwhile detouring south, past weathered sandstone, to gain great views of the Sea Cliff Bridge from an unusual vantage point.

3 Return to the pool and climb a flight of steps to Leeder Park and walk left on Patterson Road and then left back onto Lawrence Hargrave Drive and the approach to cantilevered Sea Cliff Bridge.

4 The bridge walk has become so popular that off-road parking has been provided at each end. You can read about the bridge's construction courtesy of information boards. From the far end walk uphill on the shared footpath and cycleway and pass the Clifton School of Arts, built when the mining village prospered. Detour left into Moronga Park where benches provide shaded views down to the coast.

5 Head back on the footpath and pass the boarded-up Clifton Hotel, a victim of the lengthy road closure before the bridge was finished. Pass the rail station on your right and then Scarborough's primary

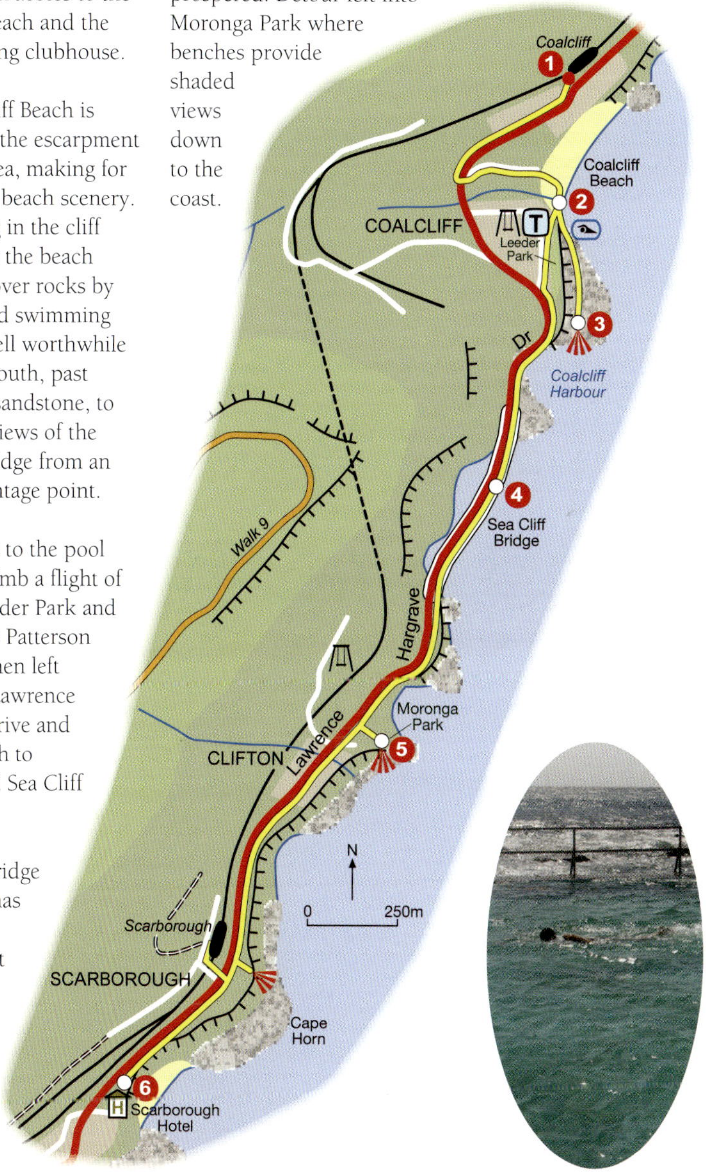

school on your left. Detour left at some bollards to an overgrown path which you can descend a short way for views down to Cape Horn and an unnamed beach. Back on the road, you'll soon reach the Scarborough Hotel.

6 A board on the hotel's exterior provides interesting reading. The hotel's Seascape café-restaurant provides a spectacular setting for refreshments – either indoors or in its garden – before returning to your car or backtracking to Scarborough station.

Illawarra environment – Sea Cliff Bridge

Since opening in December 2005, the 665-metre-long Sea Cliff Bridge has become an iconic tourist magnet. Lawrence Hargrave Drive used to follow a cliff-hugging stretch that was frequently closed by rock-falls and after an embankment slip in August 2003 it was considered too unsafe to reopen. The visually stunning bridge is cantilevered out above the Pacific Ocean, running parallel to the cliff line but out of reach of any falling rocks, and is one of only seven such bridges in the world! From the bridge, dramatic coastal views are available both north and south. At each end of the bridge are numerous inscribed padlocks locked to the guard railings, commemorating loves and friendships.

11 Wombarra to Thirroul

Avail yourself of a short, scenic rail trip for this delightful coastal walk connecting the beaches of Northern Illawarra's coastal villages. A feature of this foreshore walk is the many secluded tidal swimming pools along the extensive rock shelves; the beaches at Scarborough, Coledale, Austinmer and Thirroul are also patrolled in summer. Depending on the conditions, you can make your way over or around the various low headlands, while the cliffs of the Illawarra Escarpment provide a stunning backdrop.

At a glance

Grade: Easy/medium

Time: 2.5 to 3 hrs

Distance: 8 km one-way

Conditions: Avoid in high seas; high tide options south of Coledale

Getting there:

Train: Board at Thirroul station; alight at Wombarra station

Car: Park near Thirroul railway station and catch a train to Wombarra

Walk directions

1 From the northern end of Wombarra rail station, turn right into Morrison Avenue, left into Lawrence Hargrave Drive and first right into Monash Street to reach Illawarra Park at the back of Scarborough Beach.

2 Walk south along the beach and around the rock platform at Noonys Gulf. The igneous intrusions are from a long extinct volcano. You'll pass rock baths at little Wombarra Beach and then continue on rock – dry at low tide but requiring a bit of rock-hopping – all the way to Coledale Beach and its beachside camping ground. The boulders passed along the way are fascinating and include smoothed sandstone, delicately seamed with oxides.

3 South of Coledale Beach, sand gives way to rock as you pass Coledale tidal pool and then round a headland lined with new houses to reach Sharkeys Beach, lined with Norfolk pines and popular with surfers. A colourful mural adorns the toilet block at the beach's southern end.

4 Walk around Brickyard Point (or over it through Tuckerman Park at high tide or if you want to detour to the Headlands Hotel for refreshments with a fine coastal view) to reach an unnamed beach before rounding the low Bells Point headland. Again, there is a high-tide path option.

5 A low coal seam at the base of the cliff north of Austinmer Beach was spotted by survivors of the *Sydney Cove* in May 1797. The wretched party camped on the beach on their eight-week trek north to Sydney and made a fire from coal found on the beach. Today, there are

usually coal pebbles at the water's edge. There was once a jetty for coal transportation south of Thirroul and the tide-smoothed pebbles are probably spillage from decades ago. Austinmer Beach is a popular destination, with a playground and tidal pools. There's a popular café across the road and a take-away. The next rock platform is easily traversed but, for variety, you might take the headland footpath from the changing shed near the pools.

6 The path traverses Slade Park between cliff and houses with good views over the rock platform. When the railing stops, a narrow footpad descends left off the path through vegetation to the beach. Leave Thirroul Beach towards its southern end, near the Olympic pool in Thirroul Beach Reserve.

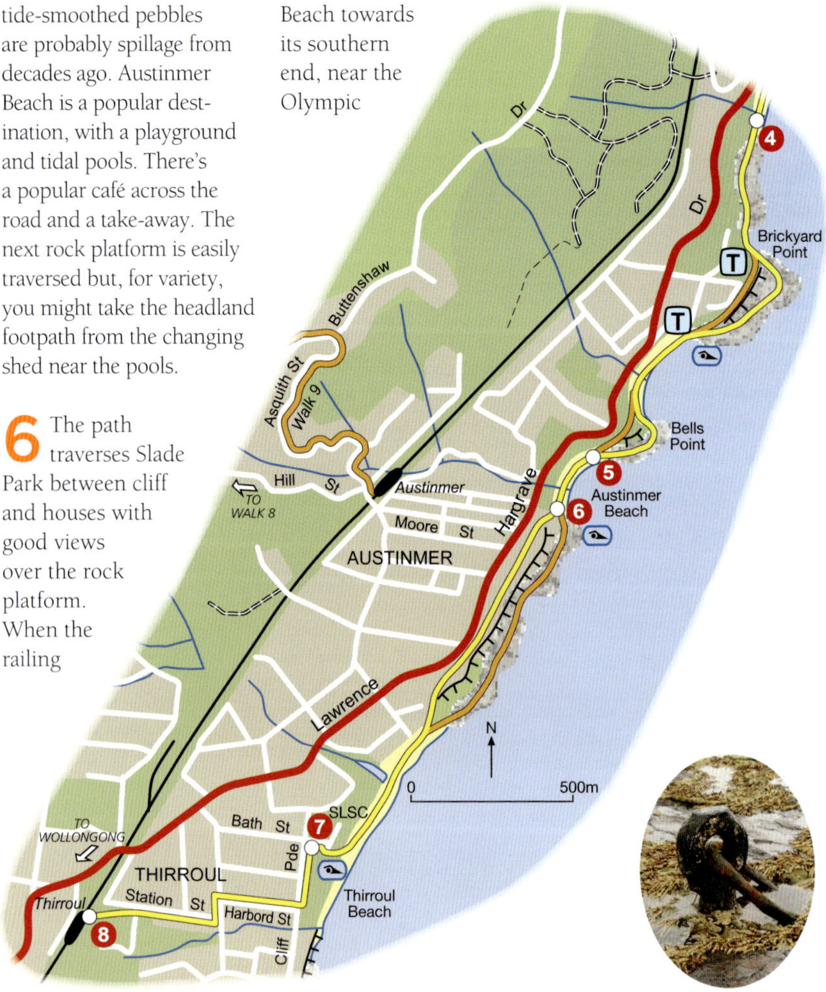

Walk variation

This walk can be linked up with the last part of walk 10 by continuing south on Lawrence Hargrave Drive after visiting the Scarborough Hotel and turning left into Monash Street for Scarborough Beach, then proceeding from waypoint 2. Of course you can finish the walk early at Coledale or Austinmer, by walking to their respective stations. For more coastal walking, you can continue south from Thirroul to McCauley's Beach and Bulli (Sandon) Point from where a shared footpath/cycle track heads through parkland, parallel to the coast all the way south to Wollongong.

7 Unless you want to detour to Thirroul's shops and cafés via Bath Street, walk south on Cliff Parade, right into Harbord Street, left then soon right into Station Street, walking through Thomas Gibson Park to reach Thirroul rail station.

8 Catch a train home or return to your car.

Illawarra history – Thirroul's visitors

From aboard Cook's *Endeavour* in 1770, Joseph Banks noted the Cabbage Tree Palms dotting the area's rainforest: Thirroul derives from *thurrural*, said to mean 'valley of the Cabbage Tree Palms' in the local Aboriginal tongue. Palms would have been largely replaced by miners' cottages by the time celebrated English novelist D.H. Lawrence rented a seafront house in Thirroul in 1922. He and his young wife Frieda stayed at *Wyewurk* (3 Craig Street in Thirroul) between May and August and there he wrote most of his 'Australian' novel Kangaroo. A brief excerpt shows how powerfully Lawrence was affected by the seascape he encountered:

He liked the sea, the pale sea of green glass that fell in such cold foam. Ice-fiery, fish-burning. He went out onto the low flat rocks at low tide, skirting the deep pock-holes that were full of brilliantly clear water and delicately coloured shells and tiny, crimson anemones. Strangely sea-scooped sharp sea-bitter rock floor, all wet and sea-savage.

Winged Figure on Mount Keira

Around Wollongong

Wollongong is the third largest city in NSW and a surprisingly walkable one at that. There is plenty of easy, level ambling through its extensive parkland and around pleasant wetlands, including Puckey's Estate and the delightful Botanic Gardens. The seascape north of Wollongong is an attractive stretch of beaches and shore platforms, with a cycle/walk path running its length. To the south more attractive coast abuts the industrial hub of Port Kembla, with a fine view out to Big Island, the largest of the Five Islands. Just inland, another path for cyclists and walkers encircles much of Lake Illawarra and offers good opportunities for watching birdlife. Those seeking more elevated vistas can head for the hills, as the Escarpment nearby contains three prominent features: Mt Keira, Mt Kembla and Brokers Nose or Corrimal.

It was the rainforest on these slopes here that alerted early colonists to the area's natural wealth and there is plenty of history here to be discovered. Today, this section of the Illawarra is undoubtedly well settled but, as a benefit, almost all of the following walks can be easily reached by public transport.

12 Bellambi Lagoon

Extending some 13 kilometres along the coastal plain from Wollongong to Thirroul is a shared path for walkers and cyclists. This walk takes advantage of a short section between Towradgi and Bellambi Creeks – both of which pool as wetlands near the coast – and a fine stretch of sand and rock shoreline to form a surprisingly rewarding circuit. At low tide there are incentives to potter on the rock platform and there will be plenty to interest bird lovers along the way.

At a glance

Grade: Easy

Time: 2 hrs 30 mins

Distance: 7 km circuit

Dogs: On leash

Conditions: Best at low tide

Getting there:

Train: Corrimal station is 1 km west of waypoint 7, along Murray Rd

Bus: Premier 3/8 runs close to the whole route

Car: North of Wollongong, leave Northern Distributor east on Towradgi Rd; turn left into Pioneer Rd, cross Towradgi Creek and turn right into Lake Pde, park at the end

Walk directions

1 Cross a grassy area and follow a beach path over the sand dunes, passing an observation tower for lifesavers. From Corrimal Beach (patrolled in season), you gain a good view south beyond Flagstaff Hill to Port Kembla headland and the Five Islands. Walk north on the wide beach to the Bellambi Lagoon outlet, usually closed to the sea.

2 You are unlikely to be alone for this section, as the 'off-leash' area attracts lots of dogs (as well as their owners). Continue on, below the vegetated dunes that make up Bellambi Recreation Area, perhaps pausing to watch for shore-birds on the rocks at Sandspit Point. Ahead are the rocks of Bellambi Reef. On 28th April of 1770, Captain Cook's crew needed water and a lowered longboat headed for Flat Rock, two kilometres north. A change of wind threatened to push the *Endeavour* onto Bellambi Reef and Cook's first attempt to land on the east coast was abandoned: the Endeavour proceeded to Botany Bay.

3 Bellambi Point has an interesting rock platform and you might want to spend time investigating if the tide permits. Rounding the point, you briefly lose the views inland of Mount Kembla and Mount Keira but one opens up of the entire northern Illawarra. Pier stumps are reminders of the long jetty that was used to load steam colliers with coal more than a hundred

years ago. When you reach Bellambi Harbour and the boat ramp behind the breakwater, cross the car park and continue along a short beach and more rocks, over a platform, sand and pebbles to reach a playground and sea baths.

4 A cycle/walkway passes here, and there are BBQs, shelters and a musical toilet! Drop down to Bellambi Beach (also patrolled in season) and walk a few hundred metres to a sandy path off the beach to regain the paved path by the narrow outlet of Bellambi Creek.

Limpets

Sea stars

Oulactis mucosa

Waratah anemones

Illawarra environment – Intertidal life

At first glance, most rockpools or tidepools don't seem to offer that much in the way of wildlife. But look again (ideally with polarised sunglasses) and things start to appear. That pink or orange stain on the side is probably an encrusting sponge: the simplest form of cell republic in the animal world and one that has survived unchanged for over 500 million years. There will usually be bits of what we collectively dismiss as 'seaweed' but close inspection will often reveal an array of types: Neptune's necklace with its beads of air bladders, bright green sea-lettuce or, more common in shaded pools, delicate red coralline seaweed.

If you stay still long enough you might think some weed moves independently: it may be a small seaweed crab that has cloaked itself with local weed as a disguise. If you're luckier still it could be a sea hare, a shell-less gastropod that moves into shallower water to lay eggs. Other gastropods are easier to spot: periwinkles, conniwinks and black nerites leave curious trails as they meander around, grazing on algae. Limpets stay put during the day but gad about at night.

Creatures that prefer moving water are more likely to be found in channels in the rockshelf or under ledges. Carnivorous sea anemones just look like blobs when low tide exposes them to the air but when covered by water they extend their tentacles in the hope of catching passers-by. Blood-red waratah anemones are the most eye-catching, but green ones have a certain charm and *Oulactis mucosa* – which glues on shell fragments as camouflage – deserves extra points for effort. If you're lucky, you might encounter sea-stars, which can range from a five-armed version the size of a 50-cent-coin to the larger spurred sea-star, which has eight arms and comes in a wonderful array of colours.

Of course, the richest rock shores are those that haven't been disturbed by humans. So, with this in mind, avoid treading on marine animals and plants, and leave everything where you found it. For your own safety, be aware which way the tide is flowing and watch out for rogue waves.

5 Cross the footbridge here, pausing to look for swamphens, dusky moorhens or other waterbirds in the tranquil creek. Now head back on the cycle path, passing the surf lifesaving club and the playground once again. Cross the road leading to the sewage works on the headland and continue south, through Bott Drive Reserve, to walk between backyard fences and a stand of swamp oaks. The path touches Birch Crescent briefly and then veers left down to the lagoon.

6 The coastal wetland of Bellambi Lagoon is particularly attractive in the early morning or late afternoon. With its tiny islands and extensive reed beds, it's a haven for waterbirds and a popular spot for birdwatchers, with seats provided on the grassy banks. Beyond the outlet, the cycle/walkway takes a sharp right turn along Murray Road and the perimeter of a holiday park.

7 At the corner of the park follow the path left (unless you need refreshments from the café further along Murray Road) into a strip of conserved native vegetation. Cross a footbridge over an arm of Towradgi Creek and return to your start point, unless you want to detour south for 500 metres to look for the 1881 wreck of the *Queen of Nations*, visible at low tide some 60 metres off the shore just north of Towradgi Point.

13 Brokers Nose / Corrimal

Brokers Nose (or Corrimal to the Dharawal people) enjoys what is possibly the finest outlook of all the viewpoints dotted along the Illawarra Escarpment and that's saying something. This 440-metre promontory was probably named after an early settler called John Brooker, though some like to claim it was because poor (broke) miners took their families up for picnics. The challenge of reaching the summit from below will make the views even more memorable and this loop walk has the added interest of passing through a disused colliery and a fine stand of sub-tropical rainforest.

At a glance

Grade: Medium/hard

Time: 4 hrs

Distance: 12.5 km loop

Ascent/descent: 400 m / 400 m

Conditions: Beware mountain-bikers on weekends; one extremely steep ascent: walking poles are useful; lower track muddy after rain

Getting there:

Train: Towradgi station is 2 km east

Bus: Green's #2 from Wollongong stops on Towradgi Rd/Princes Hwy

Car: North of Wollongong, leave Northern Distributor west into Towradgi Rd; cross Princes Hwy into Caldwell Ave and turn third right onto Meadow St, left on Keira St, right on Corrimal St and left onto Hawthorn St, park at the top of the hill

Walk directions

1 Walk around the gate: a sign advises that you are walking through privately owned property (at your own risk) and warns of possible hazards. A sealed road takes you steadily uphill on a forested ridge en route to the disused Corrimal Colliery. Half way up, go through an open gate and soon contour left below a rainforested slope. The road swings left across a creek.

2 Reach the level clearing of the Corrimal Colliery, where activity ceased in the 1960s. Dead lantana thickets are a sign that bush rehabilitation is in progress here and there's a good view up to the bluff of Brokers Nose and its tower. The mine portal has been grilled and capped with cement; you'll also find culverts, rail tracks and a turntable. The now unsealed road continues southwest steeply uphill through two gates and beneath powerlines where you get a view over Wollongong. The second gate marks the boundary of the Illawarra Escarpment State Conservation Area (IESCA).

3 The trail bends sharply right (north), once more under the powerlines and through the rainforest of the lower escarpment slopes, replete with tall cabbage tree palms and red cedar trees. Some 550 metres from the bend, past a churned up section of trail, look for rusted metal power poles in the forest on both sides of the trail. A few metres on, an inconspicuous footpad climbs the bank left.

4 Take this path which soon broadens into a dirt track, following old power poles very steeply uphill. After 300 metres (it seems like more!) you'll suddenly emerge onto the escarpment plateau at a grassy saddle. There's another view over Wollongong and a view west over the broad sedgeland gully of Rocky Creek.

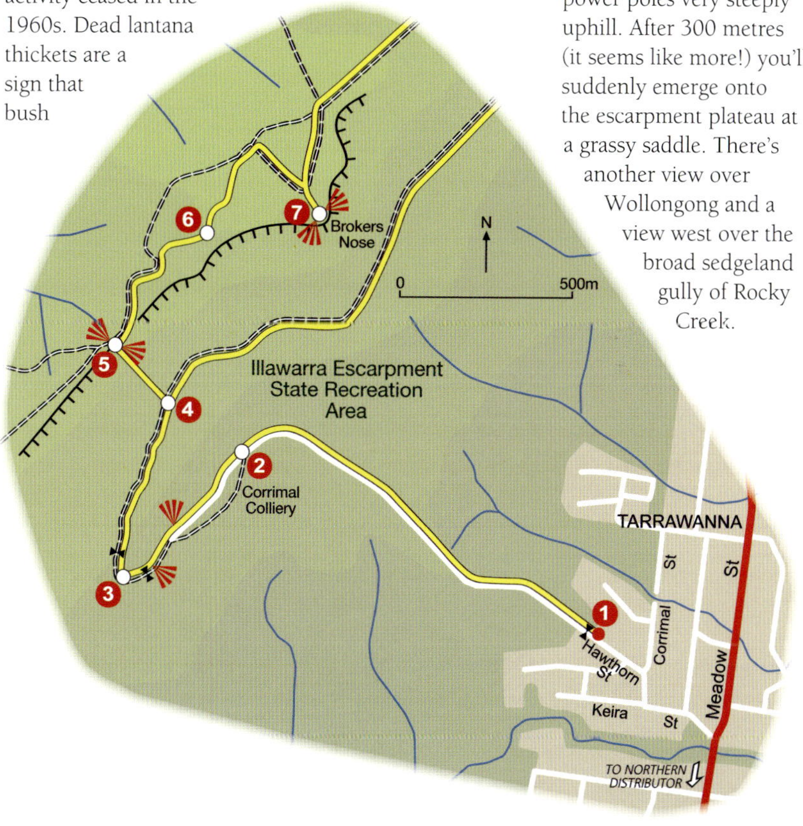

5 Follow the ascending ridge track (linking Mount Ousley Road) right; it soon becomes a 4WD service trail, winding through tall forest of blackbutt and – higher up – silvertop ash. After a right hairpin bend, the trail becomes more eroded. Just after a shortcut path rejoins from the right, take a second footpath branching off right through bracken and open forest towards the scarp.

6 Soon you'll reach a large rock sprouting a beautiful birds-nest fern, beyond which are glimpses of the coast. The path winds gently uphill through drier forest and orange lichen-stained sandstone outcrops, before rejoining the service trail near the summit. Soon turn right at another junction on a broad track heading towards the Brokers Nose broadcast tower.

7 The cliff-top beyond the tower is a perfect lunch spot with room to share the views. And what views! The whole coastline is on display, from Royal National Park all the way south to Bass Point, while the escarpment stretches from Mount Keira and Mount Kembla south to Saddleback Mountain. Directly below, a swathe of dark green forest suddenly gives way to suburban Wollongong and the waterways near Bellambi Point (featured in Walk 12) are on display. Before leaving, you might examine the 120 years' worth of names carved by picnickers. Follow the path north below some powerlines; it leaves from the perimeter fencing of the broadcast tower and merges with the main service trail where the lines turn northeast. The trail, mostly good, is steep, eroded and braided in places as you descend.

8 After a flatter stretch, the trail joins a major fire trail at a hairpin bend. Detour left briefly to view reflections in a large tree-fringed pond formed by a dammed creek. Continue on the service trail past an old mast and a power pole to another junction; the main trail heads left but you should keep ahead, rounding a locked gate to begin the steep descent of Rixons Pass.

9 At a signed junction turn right onto the Lower Escarpment Fire Trail. It is likely that this track follows a part of the historic 1815 Throsby Track which breached the escarpment south of present-day Bulli Pass and was the first land route for Europeans into Wollongong. In its early days, horses had to be led and carts

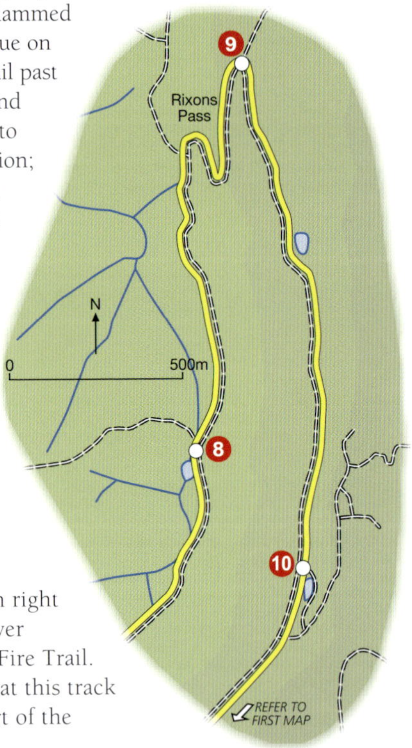

roped down the mountain. It's now easy walking through delightful rainforest as you traverse the slopes below Brokers Nose; be aware of weekend mountain-bike warriors.

10 Keep right at a fenced reservoir, ignoring two left-branching tracks. Half a kilometre further on re-enter the IESCA at a gate and, in just over a kilometre, you'll pass your earlier side-path at waypoint 4. Retrace your steps to the start point less than 2½ kilometres away – almost all downhill!

Illawarra history – The romance of red cedar

European settlement of the Illawarra would have been a much more stately affair if it had not been for the attraction of the cedar that flourished in the region's moist alluvial and volcanic soils. These tall trees were especially plentiful in the Jamberoo-Kiama district but giant specimens were common on the slopes above Wollongong. The richly coloured timber was prized for cabinet-making and lured a rough assortment (often escaped convicts) into the difficult terrain around 1810.

The deciduous cedar could be located in spring by the copper-red new leaves; in winter its bare branches stand out on the skyline. Timber was hauled out on bridle tracks and the cedar-getters lived in harsh conditions but the rewards were great. Trees were cut down in such a frenzy that, in 1819, cedar-getting was restricted by law. Nonetheless, when Governor Macquarie visited the Illawarra in 1822 he lamented that most of the red cedar had already been removed. Timber-getters turned their attention to other trees in the forest. Today, red cedars are springing up anew but it will take many years for them to reach the great size of their predecessors.

14 Wollongong's history

The city's name is thought to derive from an Aboriginal word meaning 'the sound of the sea' and you'll be hearing plenty of it on this walk. While it starts near the present city centre, this route quickly heads for the harbour that served the young settlement as a link to the outside world. This is an excellent walk to linger over and there are plenty of opportunities for refreshments and sustenance along the way!

At a glance

Grade: Easy

Time: 2-3 hrs

Distance: 5 km loop

Conditions: Great in all seasons

Getting there:

Train: Station is 900 m west of start, along Burelli St

Bus: Free shuttle bus 55 stops at start and by Osborne Park at end

Walk directions

1 Start this walk on Burelli Street in Civic Plaza, where the performing art centre houses the Merrigong Theatre Company. The name *Merrigong* appears in early European accounts of exploration of the Illawarra and is thought to derive from the Dharawal word for the nearby escarpment. On the other side of the square is a huge *trompe l'oeil* depicting the original 1927 façade of the Town Hall.

Take the covered lane at the top of the plaza and then turn right into Crown Street. In the distance you can see the stand of the WIN stadium before you turn left into Corrimal Street and then right into Market Street.

2 The grand building a short way along was, in 1882, the post office; today it is the Illawarra Museum: a good place to learn some local history, although opening hours are short. Cross the road to stroll

diagonally through pleasant Market Square, the town centre until the arrival of the railway drew commercial activity towards the station. A plaque midway on the left of the path commemorates Dr Charles Throsby who, with the help of Aboriginal guides, made his way off the escarpment via a pass near Bulli (see Walk 13) to graze

cattle hereabouts in 1815. His stockmans' hut stood a short way along on the corner of Harbour and Smith Street where you'll find another plaque to mark where John Oxley met and negotiated land grants with the new settlers in 1816. Continue on down the hill, now on Harbour Street, towards the water.

3 The elegant sandstone building on the right is the 1858 Court House, which has also seen service as a customs house and army headquarters. Cross to the foreshore park where you'll find a café and toilets and a fine view down to Wollongong's harbour, visited by George Bass in 1797 and established as the safest anchorage along the Illawarra coastline, although much convict labour was required to save visitors from having to wade ashore at Brighton Beach. With land access off the Escarpment difficult, this was, for many decades, the transport hub of the settlement. Head east across Endeavour Drive, over the grass to visit the Vietnam War memorial, and then gain a view over City Beach and the distant chimneys of Port Kembla's steelworks.

4 Follow along a white barrier, above the Ladies' Baths (once reserved for the use of women and children) to a lookout at the tip of the headland. Out to sea are the Five Islands: in Aboriginal lore, pieces of rock thrown by a father so that his five disobedient daughters might each be banished onto one. The local indigenous word for the Five Islands – *Illawarra* – gives this region its name. Inland, looms Mt Kembla and the escarpment. At the high point of Flagstaff Hill is the Breakwater Lighthouse, still in operation. Some three hundred convicts lived in a cramped stockade on this hill while labouring on the harbour below. Later, when Australia feared a Russian attack during the 1860s, cannons were set here to protect the harbour: three remain. Take the steps down by a plaque about the coke ovens, buried beneath you.

5 Here, nimble walkers can make an interesting detour: a rough footpath right and a scramble over rocks leads down to a platform where a path through bitou bush leads to a stone wall. Beyond this and a short, steep clamber down, is a secluded rockpool known as the Nuns' Pool, one of the oldest ocean baths cut along the NSW coast. Retrace your steps and continue along the footpath between a sea wall and the wall of a lookout, then head right onto the breakwater.

6 The Old Lighthouse, built in 1871, served to guide ships into Wollongong's harbour until the development of Port Kembla required the construction of the newer lighthouse at a higher elevation. Emerging from the water nearby are remains of a steam-driven crane used to hoist produce onto ships: red cedar timber, farm produce and, increasingly, coal were all shipped regularly to Sydney. Sea traffic grew so much that enlargement of the harbour became necessary. Walk back along the breakwater and around Belmore Basin.

7 It took seven years to dig out from solid rock, but the basin was opened in 1868 and allowed 3,000 tons of coal a day to be exported. However, Port Kembla took over as the major port and today Belmore Basin is home to a fishing fleet. You'll pass the fishing co-op as you walk around the harbour, though you might need to pause here for some fish and chips! Further around is sheltered Brighton Beach (where an enclosed 'bathing machine' once allowed ladies to swim while retaining their modesty) and, just before the swimming pools

Make a day of it

A few steps away from Civic Plaza you'll find the **Wollongong City Gallery**, home to an impressive collection of Aboriginal, Asian, colonial and contemporary artworks, with a varied array of visiting exhibitions. Open 1000-1700 Tues-Fri; 1200-1600 on weekends; admission is free; T 4228 7500, www.wollongongcitygallery.com.au.

Keep the kids entertained with a visit to the **Science Centre and Planetarium**, run by Wollongong University. It has plenty of hands-on exhibits. Detour at waypoint 9, following the shared cycle/walking path across Stuart Park for just over a kilometre north; alternatively you could catch the free shuttle bus near Battery Park. Open 1000-1600 daily with entry fee; T 4286 5000, www.sciencecentre.uow.edu.au.

known as the Continental Pools, the route of a tramline, leading onto the breakwater.

8 This was the Mt Pleasant Tramway that linked the harbour to the mine on the escarpment. Skips of coal were drawn, first by horse, then by locomotive, until the Great Depression of the 1930s. Beyond the pools, on the left, is a stairway that can be used to shorten the walk. On the right are two rockpools cut in 1867 for the production of salt. In the 1890s they were known as Puckey's Experimental Works and used to either distil salt or purify water. Afterwards, the larger rockpool served as the Men's Pool. The old tramway now leads through a cutting and past the back of an old pavilion to reach North Wollongong Beach, popular with swimmers, surfers and coffee-sippers.

9 Beyond the surf lifesaving club, the cycle/walkway continues through Stuart Park and Puckey's Estate and those wishing to visit the Science Centre should detour here. Otherwise, turn here and walk up the ramp behind the old pavilion that brings you up onto Cliff Road. Turn left and head back south, staying on this side of the road.

10 At Battery Park you'll see two cannons and partly excavated fortifications; these are the remains of a fort built in 1890 to guard the harbour entrance. Further along, there's a boardwalk lookout with seating, offering a fine view over the city's two lighthouses and harbour. Continue on and cross the road.

11 Osborne Park contains some striking steel sculptures and more history. At the southern end are the remains of Smith Creek Bridge, constructed from timber around 1870 as part of the Mt Keira tramline. The first steam engine in the district hauled coal to the harbour from Mt Keira in 1879. This marks the end of the walk; to reach Wollongong's commercial centre, retrace your steps up Harbour Street past Market Square and the 1840s cathedral, then turn right into Crown Street.

15 Wollongong Botanic Gardens & University

Established forty years ago on land settled very early in Wollongong's history, the Botanic Gardens are now an integral part of the city. With collections of exotic and native plants, they have something to offer in all seasons, including guided walking tours for a fee (contact T 4225 2636). A visit to the neighbouring university and its pleasant, landscaped grounds provides an excuse for a coffee stop and perhaps a swim. Together, these two public spaces form a green oasis on the Illawarra coastal plain, at the foot of Mt Keira.

At a glance

Grade: Easy

Time: 2 hrs plus

Distance: 3.3 km circuit

Conditions: Much of the Botanic Gardens is wheelchair and stroller accessible

Getting there:

Bus: Free shuttle bus 55 runs via Wollongong and North Wollongong rail stations to Northfields Ave; pick up the walk circuit from there

Car: From F6 freeway, take Keiraville exit and follow signs to Botanic Gardens car park off Murphys Ave

Walk directions

1 From the car park, walk left of the tempting playground and along the right bank of the lake. Detour out onto the rotunda to admire the array of waterbirds, including dusky moorhens, purple swamphens and hardhead ducks. Make a brief detour right to look and see if the rose garden is in bloom (late winter - early spring).

2 The picturesque drum bridge or *taiko-bashi* is a replica of one bestowed by Wollongong's sister city of Kawasaki in Japan. Cross the bridge and stroll north between the bank of azaleas and the stream, although you might want to detour left to visit the woodland garden if it is in flower. Turn left onto a broad concrete track and then right onto a gravel one. Before it veers right, cross the grassy slope to the Elizabethan-style mansion.

3 *Gleniffer Brae* was built in 1939 for the family of Neville Hoskins, a pioneer of the steel industry. Today it houses the Conservatorium of Music and the strains of a rehearsal might waft out to you on the lawn. A bench seat under a magnificent fig offers a fine

view east over the city centre. Return downhill and plunge (left) into the Illawarra rainforest, passing an Illawarra flame tree on your right.

4 Keep right at a path junction and cross a footbridge. Follow this creek downstream and turn left once again on the broad track, then left again at a T-junction. This path curves around through the native open forest section: you might choose to detour right to inspect Australian dryland plants.

5 Exit the gardens, for the time being, onto Northfields Avenue, near a major bus bay. Cross the road and veer left to the western entrance of Wollongong University. Follow this road for 250 metres before turning right onto a footpath.

6 This brings you to a stream that runs between the buildings of different faculties. Follow paths weaving downstream, passing the McKinnon Building on your left, where there are food outlets. Now, with the stream on your left, you are on a section of the Janet Cosh Tree Walk. Detour left of the Biological Sciences building to view a sizeable lake – replete with eels – beyond which stretch some of the university sports grounds. The path along the lake leads to the Recreation and Aquatic Centre, open to casual visitors for a small fee, with a café open daily except Sunday.

7 Alternatively, turn right to walk between the Chemistry building and Communications Centre to reach the library, with a café downstairs. Veer left, past the *Winged Figure* sculpture by Bert Flugelman; a much larger version of this can be seen on a hillside of Mount Keira on Walk 16. There is a seat by the nearby Duck Pond, should you wish to ponder awhile. Exit the university south through the Unicentre, crossing Northfields Avenue once again and turning right to regain waypoint 5 in less than 200 metres. Head straight uphill and take the second turning left.

8 Entering the Joseph Banks Plant House can feel like stepping into a sauna but it's well worthwhile to see the bizarre cacti that inhabit it; you might also meet the resident water dragon. Continue up the hill to the Mercury Fountain and gain a view southwest of Mt Kembla. Now follow the broad path that skirts the section of flowering shrubs to reach the playground and your start point.

Illawarra environment – Satin bowerbirds

These charming birds seem to be quite at home in the Botanic Gardens forest. The first sign you'll probably notice is the call, which sounds a little like a small bomb whistling through the air. Both the dark blue male and the olive green female move furtively, hopping along a branch or darting from tree to tree. To impress the girls, the male collects blue objects and displays these around his bower, an avenue of twigs that serves as a backdrop to his strange dance which is accompanied by wheezing and whirring noises. If the trick works, a nest gets built in a nearby tree fork.

16 Mount Keira: sea to summit

Rising out of the escarpment skyline, 464-metre Mt Keira stands sentinel over the city of Wollongong. Suburbia encroaches on its lower slopes but the sheltered gullies of the upper slopes support stands of both temperate and sub-tropical rainforest. From just above sea-level, this walk to the summit combines historic and artistic interest, diverse plant communities and the reward of magnificent vistas from Summit Park. This can be done as a one-way or return walk or, better still, you can continue the walk to Mt Pleasant and catch a bus.

At a glance

Grade: Medium/hard

Time: 3 hrs

Distance: 4 km one-way to summit

Ascent/descent: 460 m / 320 m (from summit to Mt Pleasant)

Conditions: Take care crossing roads; short scramble onto summit plateau

Getting there:

Train: Nearest station is North Wollongong

Bus: Free shuttle 55 picks up at both Wollongong rail stations and sets down at Northfields Ave; from Mt Pleasant, Premier bus 6 (daily except Sun) stops at Marine Pde (near Flagstaff Hill) and the University

Car: Park near Robsons Rd/Northfields Ave junction on the boundary of Botanic Gardens and University; parking can be scarce on week days

The summit from the sea

Walk directions

1 The signed Ken Ausburn Track leaves from the western side of Robsons Road near Northfields Avenue. Ken Ausburn was the first University of Wollongong head physicist and an avid conservationist who advocated for a park to protect the Illawarra Escarpment. Climb steeply beside houses up a grassy swathe, then on concrete tiles and a long flight of steps to reach open meadow.

2 Here soars *Winged Figure*, the Lawrence Hargrave Memorial sculpted in stainless steel in 1989 by Bert Flugelman. It's part of the art collection of the University of Wollongong from where it would have once been visible before being obscured by forest regrowth. The path ascends a spur of Mount Keira to reach the Northern Illawarra Lookout, a platform with sweeping coastline views. There's a plaque here telling of the *Queen of Nations* shipwreck at Towradgi Point. A steep flight of steps leads to a flatter section where the path contours left off the spur, through a cutting of the 1861 Mount Keira coal tramway.

3 More steps take you up to the 1907 ventilation shaft of the Kemira Colliery (a name derived from Kembla and Keira); another plaque tells of the mine's history. You soon reach the Mount Pleasant management trail: for your return, note that your path's totem is not easily seen from the trail. Go left and, in a few hundred metres, through a gate to join Mount Keira Road at a hairpin turn.

4 This junction, known as Geordies Flat, is one of several joining places for the Mt Keira Ring Track walk, with a lay-by and an information board. Take the downhill (left) branch of the Ring Track signed to Byarong Park, descending to a gully before crossing the road lower down. Ascend a set of steps and swing left, now following above the road.

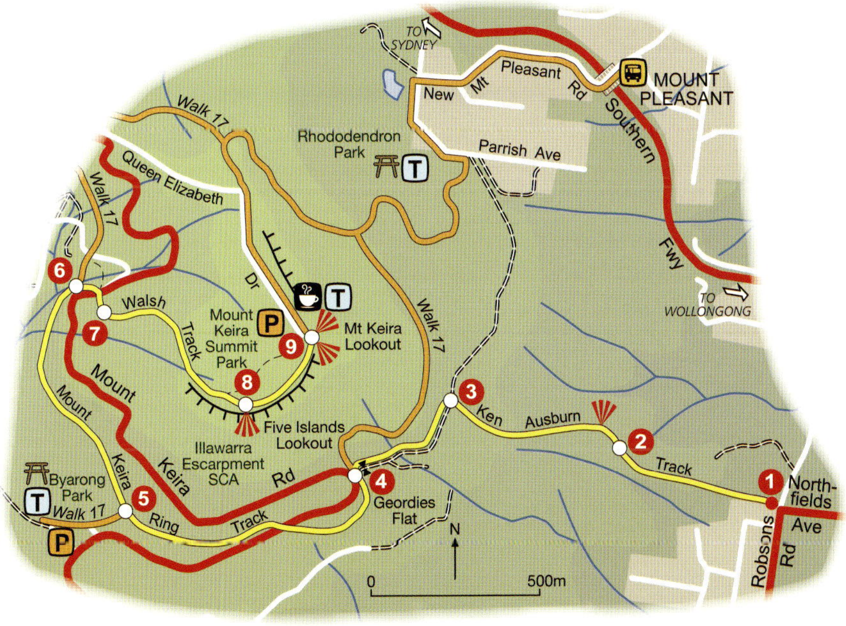

The path is lined with maidenhair fern and various exotics including ginger and lantana. Pass a rock indicating the site of the old Telegraph Camp.

5 At a Y-junction go straight ahead, signed *The Jumpers*; left takes you to Byarong Park and the start of Walk 17. Along this stretch, you can see the old cutting of the original convict-built road over Mount Keira, surveyed in 1834. A boardwalk takes you above a pond and then below a sheer rock wall where a stream crosses the path. As you contour on a forest bench, views open up of Mount Nebo, Mount Kembla and Lake Illawarra. Pass a clearing with an old bench by huge small-leaf figs: the site of *Figtrees* homestead. The path soon joins a side road to a scout camp near its junction with Mount Keira Road. Go right up to the junction, cross the main road and walk towards the gate of an access road.

6 Just to its left is the inconspicuously-signed start of Dave Walsh's Track to the summit, named after an environmentalist and long-time warden of the scout camp. Climb a steep, sheltered slope, initially through rainforest, then under a high canopy of turpentine, stringybark and silvertop ash. Keep straight ahead, where a footpad crosses, to soon climb up between some rocks. There are good views of Mount Kembla as the path swings south.

7 You'll pass left of a tumble of huge boulders, long ago detached from the cliff face; there are some climbing routes on these rocks and you can detour right, around their base, for views. Continuing upward, there's soon a short scramble through a narrow rock cleft to attain the summit plateau. It's unclear which way the track continues: head right at an unsigned junction, soon passing a termite mound and reaching a stunning viewpoint.

8 Five Islands Lookout is located at Mount Keira's southern tip, at Victoria Rocks Trig. The panorama encompasses Mount Kembla, the Port Kembla skyline and its five islands, Lake Illawarra

Mt Kembla from Mt Keira

Walk variations

For the full **'sea to summit'** experience, you could start the walk at Wollongong Harbour or Flagstaff Hill. One route takes you through Osborne Park, along Campbell Street/Throsby Drive, around Beaton Park, on a cycleway along Hay Street, then via Crawford Street, Porter Street, University Avenue and onto a cycleway through park to the eastern entry to the University to weave through its grounds and exit by the student accommodation. Allow an extra 1.5 hours and take a street map!

If you don't have two cars, there's an alternative to making this a return walk. From Mount Keira's peak, you can continue to the leafy suburb of Mt Pleasant from where you can return to Wollongong by bus. From the summit, walk down Queen Elizabeth Drive for 500 metres and fork right onto the signed footpath that links to the Ring Track. Downhill, turn right and follow the Ring Track to a path junction by a large rock and seat where you descend left, signed to Mt Pleasant. Follow yellow triangle markers through forest then veer right on a broader track that switches down to a road. Head left along Parrish Avenue, past the Rhododendron Park, and right onto New Mount Pleasant Road to cross Mount Ousley Road on an overpass. Bus 6 stops opposite Dobinson Street. Allow 1 hour.

and south to Saddleback Mountain. Back from the lookout is an installation of six bronze sculptures, fragile gunyas cast from twigs which refer to the dreamtime story about the six daughters of the west wind: Mount Keira and the Five Islands. Don't take the broad service trail to Summit Park; instead find the narrow footpad to the right, following close to the scarp and more viewpoints before emerging near a trig point.

9 Mt Keira Lookout is a popular destination, with car access, and is managed as an annexe of the Wollongong Botanic Garden. There's an extensive picnic area, with all amenities, and the nearby Mountaintop Café is open daily until 1500. The tiered lookout boasts viewpoints with binocular telescopes and a birds-eye view over Wollongong city and its northern suburbs and beaches. After soaking up the views (and perhaps a coffee), return the same way unless you've left a second car here.

17 Mount Keira Ring Track

A circumnavigation of this Wollongong landmark is one of the Illawarra's iconic walks. The well-constructed Mount Keira Ring Track follows part of the old convict-built road to Wollongong, the first cart-worthy road into the district. Mount Keira's western slopes provide fine outlooks while the northern and eastern flanks are a delightful combination of tall eucalypt forest and deep rainforest gullies. Regenerating red cedar trees are now quite common in the rainforest sections, despite the vigour with which the species was harvested by the cedar-getters of the early nineteenth century.

At a glance

Grade: Medium

Time: 3 hrs

Distance: 5.7 km circuit

Conditions: Take care crossing roads; steep and eroded sections of track

Getting there:

Bus: Premier bus 39 stops at Mt Keira Rd/Allen St, 1.4 km from Byarong Park

Car: Leave Princes Hwy on Mount Keira Rd, winding uphill; turn left into Byarong Park (signed) and park

Walk directions

1 Byarong Park was once a grazing area for the pit ponies of the Mount Keira coalmine. The park has toilets, barbeques and a spreading turpentine tree sheltering picnic tables. From this tree, walk right, across grass to a nearby information board. Behind this is a NPWS sign marking the start of the link path to the *Mt Keira Ring Track*. The path soon deposits you outside the imposing gates of a Guide Camp and continues uphill to reach a signed Y-junction.

2 Veer left onto the Ring Track. Along this stretch, you'll notice an old cutting: the path now follows the original road over Mount Keira, surveyed in 1834 by Surveyor-General Thomas Mitchell and built by convicts. A boardwalk takes you above a small pond and later below a sheer rock wall where a stream plunges over the path. As you contour the western slopes on a forest bench, views open up of nearby Mount Nebo, Mount Kembla and beyond to Lake Illawarra.

3 At a small clearing is an old bench by a couple of huge small-leaf figs, the only reminder of *The Figtrees*, a homestead which once stood here. The path soon grazes a side road to the Mount Keira Scout Camp near its junction with Mount Keira Road.

4 If you'd like to add Mount Keira's summit to the walk you should refer to Walk 16's description of *Dave Walsh's Track* here. Otherwise, the Ring Track leaves left of the Scout Camp road down some steps to cross the lush gully of Byarong Creek on stepping stones before crossing the road lower down. Continue uphill on steps and traverse a rainforest slope below the main road, where you might keep an eye and ear out for lyrebirds, echidnas and wallabies. At a white barrier gate, do not join the road but continue downhill towards electricity poles.

5 Reach a junction with Robertson's Lookout Track (see walk variation). Here you should mount the flight of railed steps to reach Mt Keira Road at a trackhead and junction with Queen Elizabeth Drive, the road to the summit. From here you get good escarpment views south to the Warra cliffs and north to Brokers Nose. Cross both roads to continue on the signed *Ring Track* down

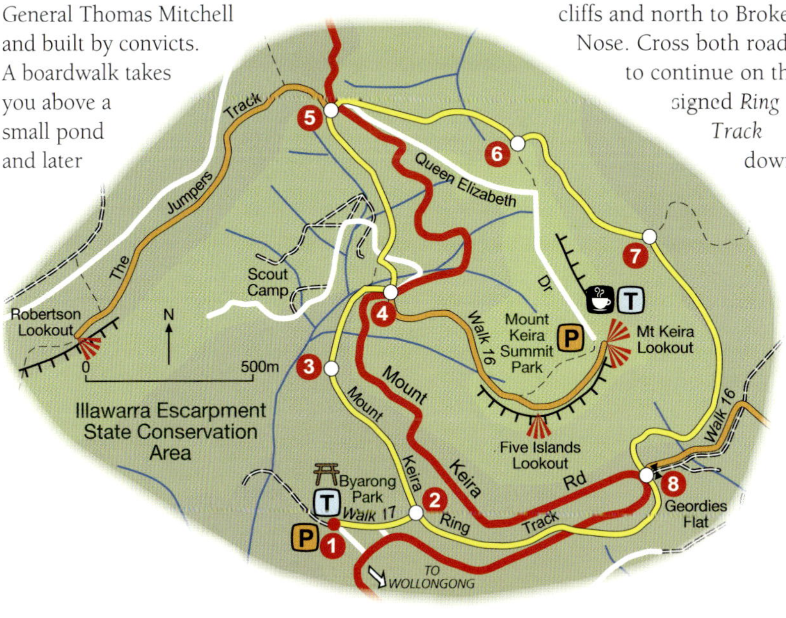

steps, descending the northern flank of Mount Keira. On this side of the mountain, lush sub-tropical rainforest gullies alternate with tall eucalypt forest. It's a delightful descent to the first such gully and a convenient seat eases the climb back out.

6 Reach a signed junction where you should keep ahead towards Geordies Flat; the path right is another way of getting to the summit. Presently you descend on stone steps through a beautiful pocket of rainforest into a grove of huge burrawangs, maidenhair, birds-nest ferns and liana vines.

7 Pass another signed junction: the path left is to the suburb of Mount

Walk variation

The 2.4-kilometre return walk to Robertson's Lookout at Warra Trig is a worthwhile diversion at waypoint 5; allow up to 1 hour. The lookout platform (wheelchair accessible via a short track from Harry Graham Drive) provides fantastic views of the coastal plain and escarpment, in particular, the sheer southern cliffs of Mount Keira, which you don't get to see while you're circling the mountain. The walk involves a steep initial climb on steps and stone before a gentle traverse of the plateau brings you to a low-key picnic spot and information board. Beyond this is a junction with the path from the road to the lookout platform, 100 metres to the left.

Pleasant. Continuing ahead on the level forest bench you presently pass left of a large cube-shaped rock split down the middle. Now descend a long flight of wooden steps to an information board where you rejoin the Mt Keira Road at a hairpin bend at the area known as Geordies Flat.

8 Fifty metres downhill, the Ring Track leaves the road left, signed to Byarong Park. Descend to a gully below the road before crossing the road lower down and climbing a set of steps. The fern-lined path swings left, now following above the road and returning you to waypoint 2, a short walk from the start.

Illawarra environment – Illawarra Flame Tree

A spectacular symbol of the Illawarra, *Brachychiton acerifolium* lights up the escarpment forest in late spring when its leaves drop to reveal brilliant, coral-red flowers. The lacy inner bark of the tall rainforest tree was used for making rope, fishing nets and even hats but the tree has survived the pressures of settlement and occasional examples can be seen on the cleared coastal plain. It shouldn't be confused with the coral tree, an exotic introduced from South America which strikes readily from fallen bits of trunk.

18 Summiting Mount Kembla

At 534 metres, Mount Kembla is the high point of the Illawarra Escarpment before it swings away from the coast further south. Unlike Mount Keira, its sister peak to the north, Mount Kembla's summit has escaped the trappings of tourism: the only incursions are a trig and an incomplete and overgrown 19th-century track, planned to carry tourists to the peak. It was originally named Hat Hill after Captain Cook remarked on the similarity of shape. Considering Mount Kembla's forbidding profile, the ascent is short and relatively easy, repaying any efforts with undisturbed forest, a series of increasingly fine district views and wildflowers in spring.

At a glance

Grade: Medium

Time: 1 hr 30 mins – 2 hrs

Distance: 3.4 km return

Ascent/descent: 180 m / 180 m

Conditions: Rocky path with one short, steep get-up; unfenced lookouts on cliffs

Getting there:

Bus: Premier bus 36 runs up Cordeaux Rd to Kembla Heights

Car: From Wollongong, take Princes Hwy to Unanderra; turn right onto Cordeaux Rd, go through Mt Kembla and keep left at a sharp bend; 1.5 km on, park at a lay-by at Kembla Lookout

Walk directions

1 Kembla Lookout is the name given to the grassy saddle between the main escarpment and Mount Kembla; electricity pylons detract a tad from the views over the Dapto Plain to Lake Illawarra and beyond. A few metres beyond the barrier gate is an NPWS information board and just beyond this a track junction: right for the Mt Kembla Ring Track (see Walk 19) and left for the Summit Track.

2 The narrow, well-formed path to the summit plateau involves a steady ascent on a west-east ridge. Walk through shaded eucalypt forest of river peppermint, white-topped box and blackbutt peppermint, a favourite haunt of lyrebirds. The old overgrown road parallels the path a few metres below you to the left; this carriageway for tourists was abandoned when sandstone outcrops were reached. Yellow metal arrows assist in path-finding, particularly on the rocky sections.

3 Skirt left of a low rock overhang, fringed with rock felt fern. Walk onto these rocks for filtered views. Further uphill, when you reach a wooden barrier, the path joins the old road fleetingly before leaving it right. Climb up by a large rock outcrop and black she-oaks - at the top you can divert right for views.

4 After the ascent through the she-oak forest, and some weaving among rocks and

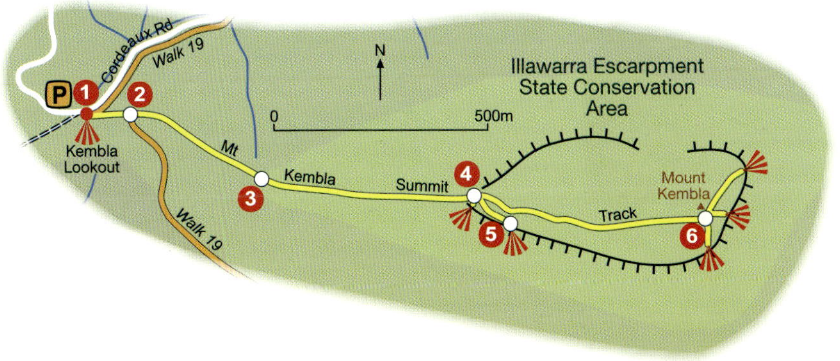

boulders, look for a scratched arrow leading you up a narrow gap in the rocks of a low sandstone scarp. Negotiating this short get-up requires use of all limbs and is the trickiest bit of the walk. A detour immediately right across the rocks takes you to your first clear view. Soon after this, another side path leads to a natural rock seat.

5 From here, the views extend over Lake Illawarra and its fringing farmland and settlements. Return to the main path. The walk across the summit plateau takes you through vegetation characteristic of poorer, sandy soils. Silvertop ash is the dominant eucalypt and there are grass trees and old man banksia, while the thick understorey includes fuschia heath, bush-pea, geebung and prickly moses – all adding interest when flowering in spring – and lomandra.

6 The track ends at the Kembla trig, marking the summit's high point. Three short footpads branch off to different viewpoints. A narrow track right (south) brings you to a fantastic view south over Lake Illawarra and Port Kembla. A footpad north of the trig leads you to a lookout point on the north-east edge of the cliffline where the views extend north over Wollongong and the north coast. After taking in the vistas, make your return on the same path.

Illawarra environment – Going, going ... gone

Europeans first discovered the koala at Mount Kembla on a scientific expedition in the winter of 1803. Specimens were collected and brought in to Sydney where they were immediately drawn by botanical draughtsman Ferdinand Bauer and described by noted botanist Robert Brown. Koalas probably disappeared from the area gradually due to the clearing of their habitat by settlers, but they were noticeably absent after a great fire of 1909 swept the Cordeaux Valley and Mount Kembla area.

19 Circling Mount Kembla

Mount Kembla is steeped in coal mining history and the area is sadly remembered for Australia's worst mining disaster in which 96 lives were lost. The Mt Kembla Ring Track circles the mountain's flanks on a level bench, passing a number of historic mining features. From the sheltered southern slopes to the more exposed eastern and northern ones, the vegetation changes from lush rainforest to delightful blue gum forest. This makes for a walk of great scenic and historic interest which you can easily combine with the previous walk to Mount Kembla's summit.

At a glance

Grade: Easy/Medium

Time: 2 hrs

Distance: 5.5 km circuit

Conditions: One steep descent; stone steps slippery when wet; watch for traffic on Cordeaux Rd

Getting there:
As per Walk 18

Walk directions

1 After pausing for the views from Kembla Lookout, round the barrier gate following the *Mt Kembla Ring Track* sign. Past an information board, head right at a signed path junction, almost immediately descending log and stone steps which zigzag steeply (with chain assistance) to the enveloping rainforest below a low cliffline. Look out for a prominent red cedar specimen by the path and admire the many cabbage tree palms, lilly pillys and giant stinging trees on the now level walk.

2 After a kilometre, the path joins a broader service trail from Farmborough Heights, open to mountain bikers. The pond on the left is a constructed dam which served as a water supply for the pit ponies that worked in the Mt Kembla colliery. The reedy, tree-fringed pond now waters the local fauna and is home to a large frog population. East of the dam, views of Mount Kembla's southern cliffs unfold and in 800 metres the track swings left (north).

3 There's another pond to the left of the track while below you to the right is the site of an abandoned farm: stands of introduced coral trees are a sign amid the regenerating bush. John Benjamin cleared 33 acres here and worked a farm from 1908 to 1953, growing vegetables, corn, fruit and grazing animals. In another

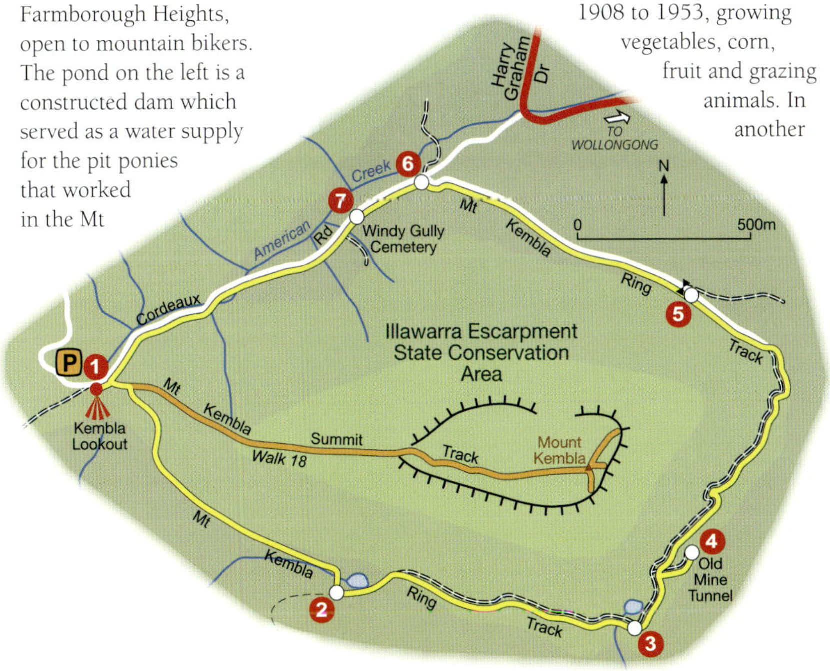

100 metres or so, hunt for a minor footpad leaving the track right (posts mark the spot) downslope. It takes you down to a level clearing from where you need to head right, to get below a stone wall where there are two grilled tunnel entrances.

4 This is the site of the shortlived Southern Coal Company Mine – poor quality coal meant it only operated from 1887 to 1890. The left hand entrance was the working tunnel that went 700 metres into the mountain; the right one was the ventilation tunnel. Linger to admire the stonework and perhaps to have lunch in the pleasant surrounds. Back on the track, you'll notice the vegetation changes quite dramatically as the track rounds the northern side of Mount Kembla: the closed rainforest opens out to a delightful forest of Sydney blue gums with their distinctively smooth blue-grey trunks.

5 Reach a gate where you leave the Illawarra Escarpment State Conservation Area; the track is now a right-of-way through private property so you shouldn't stray from it. Pass left of a photogenic old cottage to join Cordeaux Road.

6 Turn left: the 1.2-kilometre road walk back to the start is no hardship as you pass through some superb forest. After 250 metres leave the road left to inspect the cemetery at Windy Gully.

7 Here lie buried 33 victims of the Mount Kembla Mine disaster, many in unmarked graves or cairns. The Windy Gully Cemetery was finally consecrated in 2002 during the centenary commemoration of the disaster and is now recognised as a cemetery of state significance. In its beautiful forest setting, it stands as a poignant reminder of the dangers that were inherent in the early mining industry. Further along the road, a cluster of cottages built in the 1880s served as a workingmen's club, after which they became residences. The forest on the other side of the road is particularly beautiful in early autumn when the Coachwood is russet hued.

Illawarra history – Mount Kembla Mine explosion

The 1902 explosion at Mount Kembla Mine was the worst non-natural land disaster in Australia's history. Caused by the igniting of methane gas by a naked lamp, the series of coal dust explosions killed 96 men and boys on July 31, leaving 33 widows and 120 children fatherless. Most of the dead were buried in the Windy Gully Cemetery and the Anglican Cemetery down the hill in Mount Kembla village. The latter also contains a memorial to the disaster, listing the miners who died on the day as well as two rescuers who perished while saving other miners. The mine continued operating until 1970. The annual Mt Kembla Mining Heritage Festival, held at the end of July, was begun on the centenary of the disaster.

20 Port Kembla heritage

The name Port Kembla summons up one image: steelworks. Certainly, this heavy industry dominates the headland south of Wollongong but it is by no means the whole story. It was a major point of defence during the Second World War and interpretive signs make sense of what remains. Long before that, Aboriginal people made frequent use of the natural resources here and you'll find a stretch of surprisingly lovely beaches interspersed with fascinating shore platforms, as well as views of the Five Islands, which give the region its name.

At a glance

Grade: Easy/Medium

Time: 3 hrs

Distance: 5.7 km return

Dogs: On leash

Conditions: Low tide for exploring shore platforms

Getting there:

Train: From Port Kembla station follow cycle path less than 1 km along Foreshore Rd

Bus: Premier bus 65 links the station with Perkins Beach

Car: From Princes Hwy or Springhill Rd, drive east on Five Islands Rd and turn left into Darcy Rd to the coast; turn left and park before the gate at end of Gloucester Blvd

Walk directions

1 Walk north along the road into the Port Kembla Heritage Park, established to preserve the important Aboriginal, military and maritime artefacts found here. Ahead on the right are the No.1 gun emplacement and numerous tetrahedral anti-tank barriers that were placed at strategic locations during WWII. Pass the underground magazine building and the No.2 gun emplacement. The Breakwater Battery Museum is open every second and fourth Sunday of each month (small fee). Left of the museum, a circular platform offers views over the inner harbour and the industrial skyline of the steelworks to Mt Kembla and Mt Keira.

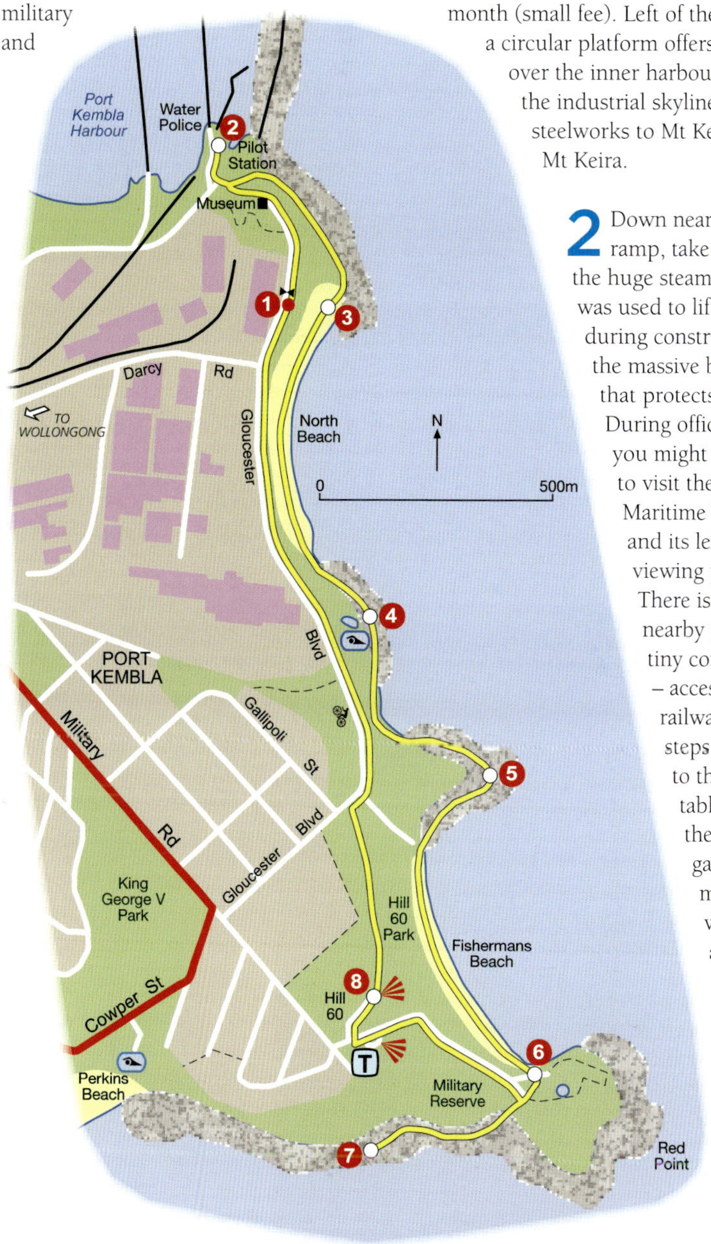

2 Down near the boat ramp, take a look at the huge steam crane; this was used to lift blocks during construction of the massive breakwater that protects the port. During office hours, you might want to visit the NSW Maritime building and its level 2 viewing platform. There is also a nearby pillbox – a tiny concrete fort – accessed via railway sleeper steps. Return to the picnic tables near the entrance gate and make your way down a footpad to the rocks and sand.

3 Walk south on North Beach with a view of Hill 60 and a cluster of islands that form part of the Five Islands; the remaining two – known as the Tom Thumb Islands after the boat that carried Bass and Flinders past in 1796 – are several kilometres northeast of you. Inland, you may (or may not) see a 198-metre-tall chimney; the stack, built in 1965, was recently found to have concrete cancer and is due to be demolished.

4 Next round a low headland where there is a disused sea pool. Shorebirds are often to be seen along here: sooty oystercatchers are regular visitors and migratory birds such as ruddy turnstones visit in summer. Raptors use the thermals overhead to hover while they scan for prey. There are two exits off the beach if the tide or swell prevent you getting around the next headland.

5 Below the headland the platform is eroded into tessellations of rectangles, triangles and diamonds. Once you're almost round the headland, you need to negotiate a narrow ledge and there's some rock-hopping to be done before you reach Fisherman's Beach. The view of Big Island (the tell-it-like-it-is name of the largest of the Five Islands) is marred somewhat by the sewage treatment works ahead. At the southern end of the beach, climb a footpad to its gate.

6 By the plant's right-hand side fence, pick up a fishers' track down onto the rocks on the other side of Red Point,

then explore east along the south-facing shoreline. Pass a small cove where a section of treatment pipe is exposed to reach a platform with dramatic trenches or dykes and some impressive block faulting. It's only feasible to continue around to Perkins Beach during low tide.

7 Retrace your steps and turn left to climb the steep road for 250 metres to a park on the left equipped with amenities. You are now on Hill 60, commandeered during WWII and riddled with tunnels and fortifications. Red Point, however, has a longer military history: it was here that the first detachment of government troops was posted in 1826 to impose order on settlement in the Illawarra and as a show of force to local Aboriginal people, for whom this landmark was sacred. From here the panorama now stretches south to take in Bass Point and Saddleback Mountain. Cross the road and wander up a footpad to the launch area for hang-gliders and paragliders, where there is an orientation table, a trig and picnic tables.

8 Take the sandy path, just left of the trig, that leads downhill to a grassy viewing area. Beyond this, the path descends on steps to the edge of a large grass landing zone, still part of Hill 60 Park. Cross the grass to Gloucester Boulevarde and walk back on the shared cycle/walkway above North Beach. As you near your start point, you pass a group of colourful dreamposts decorated with Aboriginal designs. A large midden nearby is testament to frequent use of the area by Aboriginal people over the millennia.

Out and about – Australia's Industry World

For an even closer view of the steelworks, join a guided tour through the largest manufacturing plant in Australia. The audio-assisted tour departs from the BlueScope Visitor Centre at the Northgate in Springhill Road, Coniston and takes you through restricted areas with lots of explosions and molten metal. Long trousers and enclosed footwear are compulsory but you do get the loan of a hard hat! A two-hour tour operates at 0930 on Wednesday and Friday; not suitable for children under 10; bookings essential and fee charged; T 4275 7023.

21 Hooka Point

Much of Lake Illawarra's foreshore can be walked or cycled on a dedicated path and this easy walk takes advantage of that; young children might prefer to pedal alongside. There are plenty of opportunities to see water birds, with a visit to a towering bird hide as a destination. The start/end point is by a seafood shop so fish-and-chips are an option if you build up a hunger on the walk.

At a glance

Grade: Easy

Time: 1 hr 30 mins

Distance: 4.6 km return

Dogs: Permitted on leash

Conditions: Little shade

Getting there:

Bus: Premier bus 34 from Wollongong via Unanderra station passes the start

Car: From Princes Hwy south of Wollongong, follow Northcliffe Dr to the lake shore and park in the car park at Berkeley Harbour, opposite George St

Walk directions

1 The boat harbour is protected by a rocky breakwater, a popular roost for gulls and pelicans. Walk around the artificial bay to the right of the seafood outlet to reach a picnic shelter. A dyke has been built here to create a separate lake where Budgong Creek enters Lake Illawarra and it's possible to walk along the gravel-topped embankment, enjoying the different birds attracted to the fresher water.

2 At the end, by a gate, turn left onto the cycle/walkway and continue around Tuggerah Bay through Holborn Park. Across Lake Illawarra you can see the raised plateau of Barren Grounds ending in the point of Mount Noorinan, with Saddleback Mountain to its left.

3 A long jetty offers possibilities for fishing – bream and flathead are to be caught here – and there is a playground just nearby. Others will be content to watch ibis wading over the tidal mudflats. Offshore you can see Gooseberry and Hooka Islands, which together make up Berkeley Islands Nature Reserve, protected by the NPWS. Although they have been exploited, the islands still support remnants of sub-tropical rainforest, including huge Moreton Bay figs, giant stinging trees and Illawarra flame trees.

4 Continue along the path into Hooka Point Park, passing decorated blocks of sandstone. Keep left when the path forks and rises gently up a hill. Left of the path – set among swamp oaks and eucalypts – is an observation tower.

5 Climb the tower steps for a great view over the lake. If you've brought binoculars, this is also the spot to watch for visiting birdlife. The onward path

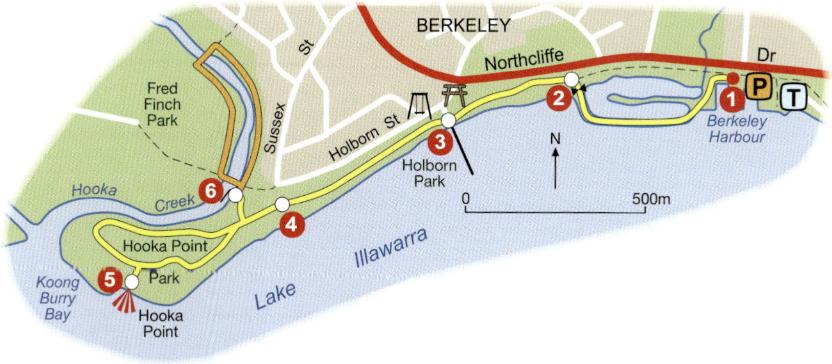

loops around the point of land to Hooka Creek, its banks supporting mangroves and lovely swamp paperbarks or melaleucas. Once around the loop, detour left on a path towards a bridge over the creek.

6 Walk the length of the jetty; its boards are incised and tiled with Aboriginal motifs. It's possible here to add on a short loop by crossing the bridge to Fred Finch Park and re-crossing Hooka Creek some 500 metres upstream to return on the bike path. From the jetty, return to the park entrance at waypoint 4 and back along the path to Berkeley Boat Harbour.

Illawarra history – King Hooka

Charley Hooka was the European name for Kerwune, an Aboriginal leader whose territory included the western shore of Lake Illawarra, with a camp on the banks of Hooka Creek. In 1842, he led his warriors to battle against an incursion by Aboriginal men from south of the Shoalhaven River. The local tribe was victorious but at great cost of life: King (or *Kana*) Hooka was buried on a mainland point near the suburb that bears his name.

Killalea coast

Around Shellharbour

The Shellharbour region south of Wollongong is attracting ever-increasing numbers of residents but there are still plenty of natural areas to be enjoyed. At its northern boundary, the entrance to Lake Illawarra features numerous small islands worth exploring, while to the south the Minnamurra River makes a picturesque exit to the Tasman Sea. The coastline in between is spectacular, with attractive beaches and wild headlands wrought by volcanic activity. Inland, Macquarie Pass breaches the Escarpment along a route long used by Aboriginal people and the regenerating rainforest is quietly obliterating signs of early attempts to disturb it.

These diverse environments offer habitats for a variety of birds and animals, so walkers might want to take a pair of binoculars with them, plus a snorkel and mask if visiting beautiful Bass Point. Premier Illawarra buses link the region with Wollongong and Kiama and can be used to access several of the coastal walks.

Macquarie Rivulet

22 Lake Illawarra Entrance: two islands walk

Lake Illawarra was once a deep, freshwater lagoon. When sea levels rose some 6,000 years ago following the last great ice age, the lake became a broad bay that was gradually cut off from the sea by the sand bar that today forms the Windang Peninsula. In 1796, Matthew Flinders named the lake 'Tom Thumb's Lagoon' after his ship; it's thought that the lake entrance is Flinders' 'Canoe Rivulet'. This easy waterside wander from its tip will appeal to all ages, with swimming opportunities at a patrolled beach or in the safe shallows of Lake Illawarra. Picnic Island is a fantastic 'hide' for birdwatchers and Windang Island caters for those with a geological bent as well as for the photographer hoping to capture great coastal scenery.

At a glance

Grade: Easy

Time: 2 hrs 30 mins

Distance: 6.5 km one way

Conditions: No shade; tide affected

Getting there:

Bus: Premier 51/53 from Wollongong stops on the north side of Windang Bridge

Car: Drive south to Windang from Wollongong; immediately before Windang Bridge, turn left onto Fern St; turn right into Waratah St, passing the tourist park, to reach the Windang SLSC car park at the road end

Walk directions

1 Head to Perkins (or Windang) Beach via the sand path behind the SLSC and walk to Berrwarra Point, the southern tip of the Windang peninsula, which stretches some 7 kilometres north to Red Point. It seems that sand is no longer accumulating here and the beach is slowly being eroded. Stroll around the sandy entrance to Lake Illawarra.

2 When you reach the northern breakwater you'll pass a fenced site designed to protect shorebirds: this is the only place in the Illawarra where the endangered Little Tern nests. Follow the sandy path to get to the Windang Foreshore Park near the SLSC. Walk through the park (which has toilets, BBQs and a playground) on a boardwalk above the inlet and then on a pebblecrete path. There's a coffee shop nearby. The path continues under the road bridge to little Edith Lacey Park.

3 Walk up some steps to cross the bridge on a footpath, keeping a watch for birdlife on the lake: over 75 different aquatic birds visit it. Once over the bridge veer right, over Pelican View Reserve, to cross another footbridge onto Picnic Island, fringed by mangroves. A sandy foot track rounds the island – a bird sanctuary – to reach a viewing platform at the island's western edge, overlooking Bevans and Cudgeree Islands. Mounts Keira and Kembla can be seen in the distance.

4 The island path returns to the footbridge, after which cross over the grass and go left on the footpath/cycleway, walking under the southern approach to the road bridge. The path goes through the extensive parkland of Reddall Reserve – a 1988 bicentennial project – boasting all amenities including change rooms and a kiosk open on weekends.

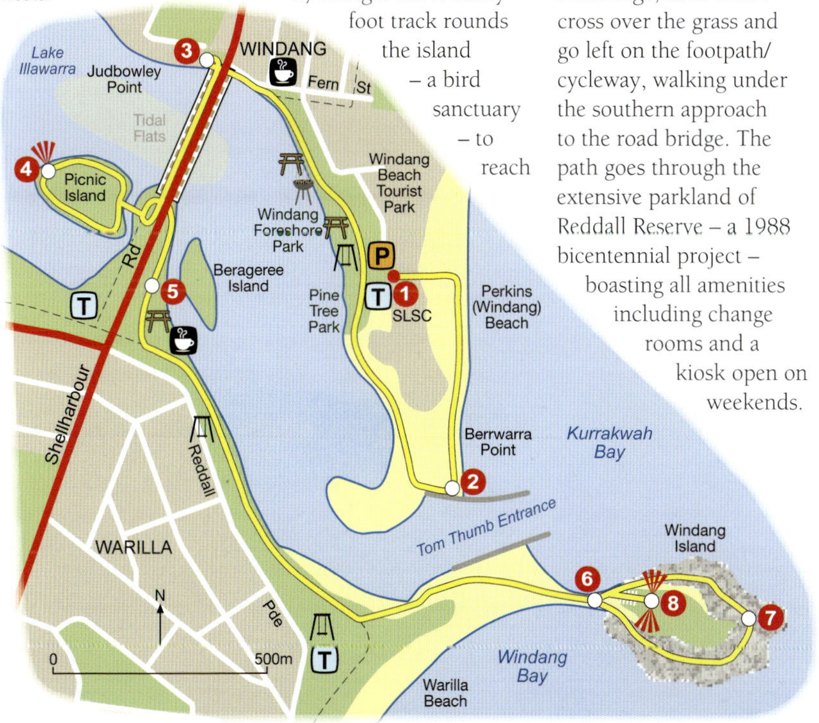

5 To the east, a shallow arm of the lake entrance is formed by the long, near-shore Berageree Island. Boats are barred from this channel, making it a safe haven for young children to paddle. Follow the southern lake entrance breakwater and sand to reach the built-up spit connecting Windang Island with the mainland at all but high tide. Take care not to get stuck on the island!

6 According to a Dreaming story, Windang Island is the abandoned canoe used by the Thurawal people to reach the continent. To your right, Windang Bay is protected by the sandspit and Warilla Beach sweeps south to Barrack Point. You'll pass a photogenic set of carriage wheels embedded in the sand; a rail line was built here in the 1890s to carry rock quarried off the island for breakwaters. Cross some purple-hued rock of volcanic origin – tufaceous sandstone – and walk around the island's shore platform.

7 On the island's far side, look out for the igneous intrusion or dyke that runs along the rock platform for 100 metres or more. Back near the sandspit, climb the wooden steps to the viewing platform for expansive coastal views.

8 To the north is the Illawarra Lake entrance with the escarpment beyond, the long sweep of Perkins Beach and the Five Islands off Port Kembla's Red Point. To the south, beyond Barrack Point,

Shellharbour is tucked in behind the Cowrie Island headland and Bass Point lies beyond, with Saddleback Mountain prominent inland. The direct return, missing out the side trips and loops, is about 2 kilometres. Alternatively, in season you could wade or swim across the shallows of the lake's entrance, well in from the breakwaters.

Illawarra environment – Walking the lake

Often referred to as the 'Jewel of the Illawarra', Lake Illawarra is one of the region's great natural assets. At 35 square kilometres, it is the second largest saltwater lake in NSW and offers opportunities for fishing, prawning, swimming, snorkelling, boating, waterskiing and windsurfing. And for walkers? Sadly, as the Illawarra's population has grown, sections of its 37 kilometres of foreshore have been affected by unsympathetic development, but there are stretches where the walker is made to feel very welcome. From Hooka Point, near Berkeley, you can follow a shared cycle/walkway clockwise around, across the lake's inlet, and as far as Yangar Point at Oak Flats. A short street walk to Albion Park rail station, a train to Unanderra and bus 34 will take you close to your start point; a walk of about 23 kilometres. Haywards Bay area is currently being developed and Yallah Bay poses an obstacle, but a full circuit of the lake may one day be feasible.

23 Shellharbour village

The small, historic port of Shellharbour should in no way be confused with the commercial centre of Shellharbour City: the former is a delightful place for a stroll. This protected cove was once known as Yerrowah and was a popular meeting place for the Wodi Wodi people. Colonial graziers and timber-getters arrived at the turn of the nineteenth century and the port was shipping out cedar from the 1820s. On this short walk you can appreciate the natural charms of the harbour and sight some local history.

At a glance

Grade: Easy

Time: 2 hrs

Distance: 5.5 km circuit

Dogs: On leash

Getting there:

Bus: Premier 53 links Wollongong station to Shellharbour Beach

Car: Leave Shellharbour Rd to turn east into Mary St at the lights; turn left at Darley St, and right into John St to reach a council car park at Bassett Park

Walk directions

1 Take the beach access path to the north of Shellharbour's South Beach. A large marina is proposed for directly south of the beach. Across the bay is Bass Point, the location of Walk 24. Turn left and walk around the point on the shore platform. The tourist park on the headland stands on a midden of shells and other inedibles, a legacy of the indigenous people who camped in the area for thousands of years. Cross the stony beach.

2 Pass the saltwater Beverley Whitfield Pool, open all year. In 1895, efforts were made to shape Shellharbour as a holiday destination: the rock baths were established and Norfolk pines planted. A short way further on are a row of old-fashioned picnic shelters. Walk around more rocks to a sand beach, backed by Little Park, and then to the pretty harbour of Shellharbour.

3 A jetty and boat store were built here in 1859 but within a few years a larger jetty was needed and the harbour entrance was deepened to allow the entry of steamers. The concrete breakwater was added in 1879. Colonies of figbirds and little corellas often roost in the ancient fig trees adjacent to the harbour. Walk around the harbour on the path to gain access to the rocks to the north. A fish-cleaning basin near the end of Towns Street often draws the interest of local pelicans: watch out when walking below their light-pole perches!

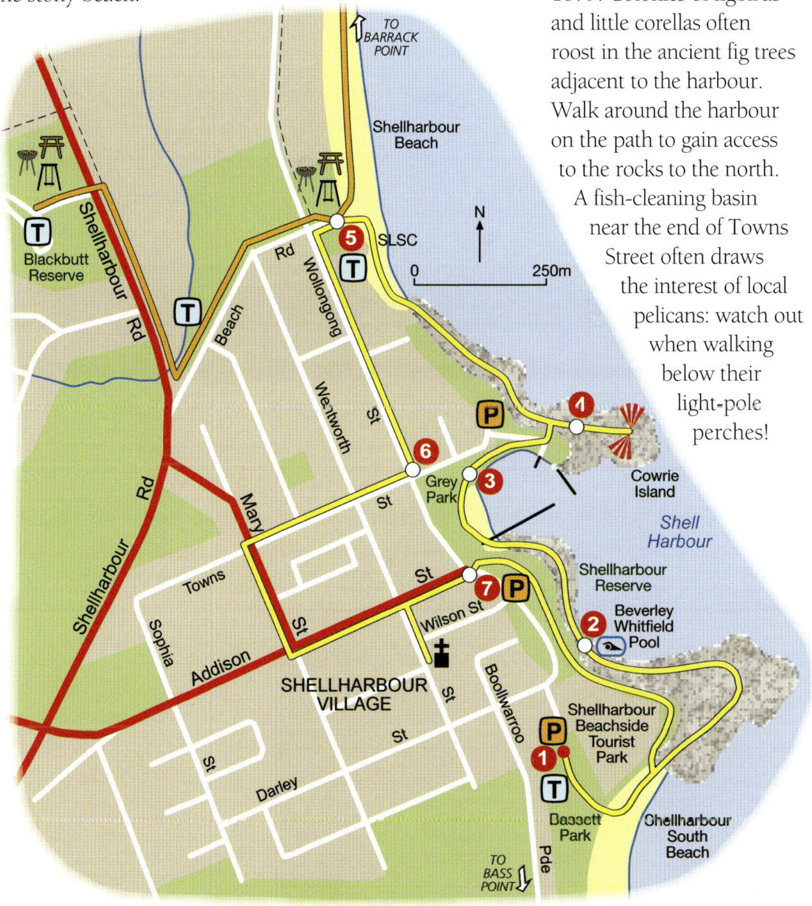

23 Shellharbour village

Leave the roadway and head right, down over the grass to the rockshelf.

4 From the tip of this point, known as Cowrie Island, there are fine views north to Port Kembla and the Five Islands, and inland to Mt Kembla and Mt Keira. On the rough path, pass the steps leading up left to the road and continue around, ignoring more steps at the southern end of the beach. Walk a short way along Shellharbour Beach to some wide steps and a ramp near the SLSC.

5 There are many options here: it's a good spot for a swim when the beach is patrolled in season and Bardsley Park has a playground. Those who want to extend the walk can continue north on the beach and explore

the bluff of Barrack Point and the inlet on its north known as Little Lake. These offer excellent locations for watching shorebirds: little penguins are sometimes sighted fishing off the headland. Nearby Blackbutt Forest is also worth a visit; see the boxed text. Otherwise, follow the footpath along Wollongong Street.

6 Turn right to walk up Towns Street, passing the Anglican church of St Pauls, built in 1886 to replace an earlier structure. Turn left into Mary Street, passing the 1871 public school and the 1865 Wesleyan chapel, then left again into Addison Street, where a memorial on the left remembers the work of Caroline Chisholm, who helped many migrant families settle in the district. On the right are the much-restored Allen's Store at No.35 and the attractive 1871 house *Windradene* on a corner. It's worth detouring briefly right along Wentworth Street to view *Stella Maris*, the village's oldest church, dating from 1861. Plaques alert you to other buildings that once stood in the vicinity and there are several cafés to be found in Addison Street.

7 Back at the seaside, continue on the path through Shellharbour Reserve and skirt the Tourist Park on a sandy path above the rock platform. This brings you back to South Beach and the access path back to the car park.

Blackbutt Forest

Out and about – Blackbutt Reserve

On a hill just inland from Shellharbour Beach is a 100-hectare reserve that contains one of the last viable remnants of coastal plain forest in the Illawarra and it offers a glimpse of what the landscape was like before European settlement. Blackbutt Reserve has various facilities scattered at its edges but the central area is bushland, criss-crossed by various trails and footpads. It is a popular spot for walking leashed dogs and for watching woodland birds. Walkers can reach it from waypoint 5 by following the cycle/walkway along Beach Road, right along Shellharbour Road and the left to climb the hill at Erwin Zatschler Drive.

24 Bass Point Reserve

Just south of Shellharbour, one rocky little headland resisted encroaching settlement and quarrying. The combined values of Bass Point – its natural beauty, cultural and archaeological features – have warranted a listing in the Register of the Australian Heritage Commission and it is indeed a special place to visit, especially if you're prepared to leave the level path. When the water temperature permits, you'll want to leave dry land altogether, but bring a snorkel and mask with you! With its diverse habitats, this is also a great location for watching birdlife.

At a glance

Grade: Medium

Time: 3 hrs

Distance: 5 km circuit

Conditions: Easy rock-hopping, one short difficult section

Finding the track

Near Shellharbour village, leave Shellharbour Road at the lights to head east down Addison Street and follow signs for Bass Point; on Bass Point Tourist Road, pass the long quarry jetty and turn left to park in a large lay-by down by a boat ramp.

Walk directions

1 A sign marks the start of the Bass Point Coastal Walk. The grassy path wanders past volcanic latite rock to soon reach Red Sands Beach, presumably named after the iron-oxide intrusions in the nearby rocks. From here, there are sweeping views of the Illawarra Escarpment and the coast from Shellharbour to Port Kembla. Behind the beach is a thicket of lantana, backed by tall coastal banksias. Around from the beach, head past a set of steps coming down from the right, then continue around onto the sand and rock-hop around to the next small cove.

2 This beach of large grey pebbles is known as The Middy. Continue on to soon pick up the main walking track to reach another tiny sand beach at Beaky Cove, backed by banksias that are frequented by honeyeaters and introduced red-whiskered bulbuls. Rejoin the path briefly and walk through stone barriers to reach the main picnic area, fringed by casuarinas.

3 There's an indigenous cultural path around this clearing. Middens on Bass Point indicate Aboriginal activity here from at least 17,000 years ago, when this area was well inland; one yielded the earliest edge-ground axe found outside of tropical Australia. At the eastern edge of the clearing, take time to inspect the Gutter: a dramatic, 40-metre-long volcanic dyke, formed when molten magma was forced into a fissure of existing rock and then

eroded away. Walk through the parking area (with tucked-away toilets) and along the road, to pick up the Shipwreck Memorial Path.

4 This monument honours those who lost their lives when Australian soldiers went to the aid of sailors aboard an American ship wrecked in 1943. At low tide, fragments of the ship can be seen off its namesake, Boston Point. Continue around the point on a stony path to another shelly beach. More rock-hopping brings you around the tip of Bass Point – named after George Bass who explored the coastline in 1796 – to the mouth of deep Bushrangers Bay.

5 Nearby, between inlet and littoral forest is a large, interesting freshwater pool. Continuing on from here requires a more difficult scramble where you traverse a side inlet while a few metres above the water. The rocks here are slippery: if it's not to your liking, turn back and retrace your steps.

6 The clear waters of Bushrangers Bay are safeguarded as an aquatic reserve and there is plenty of marine life to be seen by snorkellers and divers. The pebbly, wind-protected beach is a great spot for a picnic. You might detour up the steps to a viewing platform (also a possible exit to shorten the walk: see the boxed text). Near the bay's southern head, pass another side path, known as Fisherman's Walk. Keep rock-walking past lichen-stained latite, dotted with rockpools. Views open up south to Saddleback Mountain and the Killalea coast and you pass yet another possible exit path. Get around

Saddleback from Bass Point

Walk variation

If you tire of rock hopping, you might want to leave the shore at either Bushrangers Bay (waypoint 6) or out on the southern headland shortly after. Both these inland paths lead to the end of a dirt road. Follow the road, through a stand of littoral rainforest, back to the main picnic area, from where you can follow either the road (watching out for young drivers who like to hoon around here) or the shoreline back to your car.

another shallow bay: a grassy path leads between a frog pond and the rocks above.

7 Just after the start of Maloneys Bay, you'll reach a large dyke or chine that's impassable at water level. Backtrack a few metres to pick up a faint footpad up through the scrub. Don't go too far inland, the footpad stays close to the top of the chine to exit back onto the rocks at the other side. Watch for a mini blowhole a short way on. Just before reaching sand at Maloneys Bay, leave on a broad, stony track uphill, with the boundary of a blue metal (or latite) quarry to your left; its lease is due to expire in 2020.

8 When you reach a picnic area you'll find a short path detouring to a viewing platform over Maloneys Bay. Cross the barrier gate and walk along the broad, dirt road by grassland to reach the main road in a few hundred metres. Turn left for 100 metres and then turn right to walk down to your car.

25 Minnamurra Spit and Killalea Lagoon

It may be hard to find but Killalea State Park is worth the effort as it preserves some eight kilometres of the best coastal scenery in the southern Illawarra. At its southern tip, the Minnamurra sand spit shelters a rare patch of littoral rainforest and the northern boundary is marked by a freshwater lagoon that attracts numerous waterbirds, including flocks of black swans. The park is a popular destination for birders, surfers, picnickers, educational groups and weddings; it even offers basic camping. Here is a two-part walk (the second leg adds a degree of difficulty) that showcases the best of Killalea.

At a glance

Short circuit

Grade: Easy

Time: 1 hr 30 min

Distance: 4.5 km circuit

Long circuit

Grade: Medium/hard

Time: 4 hrs 30 min

Distance: 11.5 km circuit

Conditions: Includes scrambling and thickets; avoid at high tide or swell

Finding the track

South of Shell Cove, leave Shellharbour Road left (south) onto Bass Point Quarry Road, following signs to Killalea Park. Turn right into Killalea Drive, go through a boom gate and park at the circle at the very end of the road. The park is open daylight hours only.

Walk directions

1 From the further, west side of the turning circle, walk south over the grass, which soon becomes a mown track descending through a lantana thicket and swings left through an open rusted gate. This was once a farm and there is still much rehabilitation work to do. The Minnamurra River and rail bridge come into sight below as the ridge descent continues through swamp oak and forest red gums. It levels at a track junction; continue ahead, veering right. When you reach another Y-junction it's well worth making a brief detour right through coastal rainforest to the banks of the Minnamurra River estuary.

2 This is a tranquil spot to pause amid the large grey mangroves and swamp lilies. Across the tidal inlet, Yellow Rock Colliery can be seen dismantling the escarpment below Knights Hill. Closer to hand, you might catch sight or sound of an eastern whipbird or a black faced monarch. Back at the junction, take the other fork, which soon narrows to a footpath. At a T-junction, turn left (right is another river detour) and almost immediately right between beach dune and river estuary. At yet another junction head left, cresting the dune to reach the beach.

3 The northern end of Minnamurra Beach (known to surfers as Mystics) is where the board riders congregate but you should have the southern stretch to yourself. Walk south for 200 metres or so with Rangoon (also called Stack) Island in view, leaving again via a track

through the back dune to arrive once more at the river bank at a tiny sand beach. From here you can walk the river sand to the end of the spit – you'll need to carry your shoes except at low tide but there are few obstacles. Views across the river are to Minnamurra village and south to Minnamurra Point.

4 From the southern point, follow pristine Mystics Beach north, passing close by Rangoon Island. Dunes give way to rock and cliff as you approach the northern tip where a set of rock steps off the beach provides a short-cut to your car. This marks the end of the short and easy circuit.

5 If the swell isn't too big, continue around toward the headland of Westringia Point, named for the coastal rosemary that grows here. This involves rock-hopping some way above water level over dark volcanic latite, stained with brilliant

yellow and orange lichen. There's a clamber up and down at one point but the going is reasonably good.

6 On reaching a deep, high gulch, you have a choice: the sure-footed can walk on exposed rocks near its edge (taking great care!) to avoid an otherwise unpleasant bush bash through lantana thicket and bitou bush to skirt it. At the head of the gulch, pick up an eroded footpad ascending inland to the mown grass of the former farm. Follow the grass edge right, above the headland to pick up a footpath taking you back down to the rocks, well past the obstacle.

7 The going is easy until the first of two chines or dykes is reached. Clamber down its side to a tiny pebble beach at its head and up the other side. The second chine is even narrower but both can be rounded if you're prepared to scramble. More straightforward rock-hopping will get you to the shore platform – streaked with mineral-rich instrusions – just before Killalea Beach.

8 Also known as The Farm, this is one of the best and most popular surfing beaches on the south coast; in fact, The Farm and Mystics Beaches have recently been designated a National Surfing Reserve. Walk to

Illawarra environment – The battle for Killalea

Killalea is not a National Park but a State Park, managed by a board of trustees, and it is not immune to (over) development. A pitched battle over a proposed multi-million-dollar eco-tourism resort – 106 accommodation lodges and amenities – has raged over the last few years. The Save Killalea Alliance was formed and union green bans were imposed by the South Coast Labour Council. The chill winds of the global financial crisis helped cool the ardour of the development group for the project and in 2010 the State Government announced development plans had been scrapped. However, it could all too easily happen again; Killalea deserves permanent protection!

the eastern end of the beach and head inland on a track through the back dune to skirt above Killalea Lagoon's eastern banks. The sand dunes separating the sea and lagoon were once the site of a short-lived gold mining business in 1872 owned by Edward Killalea.

9 The track veers close to the lagoon's reed-lined bank allowing a short detour to a good vantage point for bird-watching. Well over 60 species – waterbirds, shorebirds and raptors – have been recorded here. If low water-levels expose mudflats you may see crakes, rails, dotterels, sandpipers and stilts. Out on the water look for black swans, chestnut teals, musk ducks, ibis, egrets, and many others. The path gains height and nears a quarry boundary fence where you get sweeping views of the coastline south to Kiama's Blowhole Point. Curve left behind the lagoon to reach a large, shady tree and picnic table.

10 Soon after the picnic area, leave the lagoon track for a right-branching path up a steady hill. This emerges at Frasers Picnic Area by the foundations of the old farmstead and near a picturesque but off-limits rotunda.

11 Linger awhile to take in the superb scenery. There are several picnic tables and BBQs and toilets are not far away. Cross the grassy grounds to Killalea Drive and head left on the grass verge to stroll 1.75 kilometres mostly downhill to the car, keeping straight on at both junctions.

26 Macquarie Pass Cascade Rainforest

The rugged escarpment amphitheatre of Macquarie Pass National Park is a remarkable sight to the west as you travel through the southern Illawarra. The park protects some of Australia's most southern subtropical rainforest and is named after a historic route taken from coastal plain to the highlands. This creek-side rainforest walk to a waterfall in the foothills of the park is the only officially designated walking track in the park. It's a short but beautiful stroll, especially after rain.

At a glance

Grade: Easy

Time: 1 hr

Distance: 2 km return

Conditions: Best after rain, but not during

Finding the track

From the Princes Highway, turn inland on the Illawarra Highway just south of Yallah and follow it right at a 4-way junction through Albion Park. About 9.5 kilometres from here, cross Macquarie Rivulet and park in the large bay on the right.

Walk directions

1 Cross the grass-mown picnic area to a metal signboard at the far right corner, marking the head of the Cascade Rainforest Walk. This is the first of several interpretive signs along a mostly well-graded path that makes use of an old cedar-getting trail.

2 The path soon leaves the Cascades Stream, a tributary of Macquarie Rivulet, climbing log steps to meet another track joining from the left. Descend once more to the creek and soon pass on your left a huge strangler fig in a small clearing.

3 Continue upstream – there are several places you can easily detour to the stream where maidenhair ferns grow along the bank. Most of the red cedars have long since been logged but rainforest species such as cabbage tree palm, tree-fern, liana vine, giant stinging tree, lilly pilly, coachwood and sassafras abound. In cooler seasons, the fungi can be spectacular after rain.

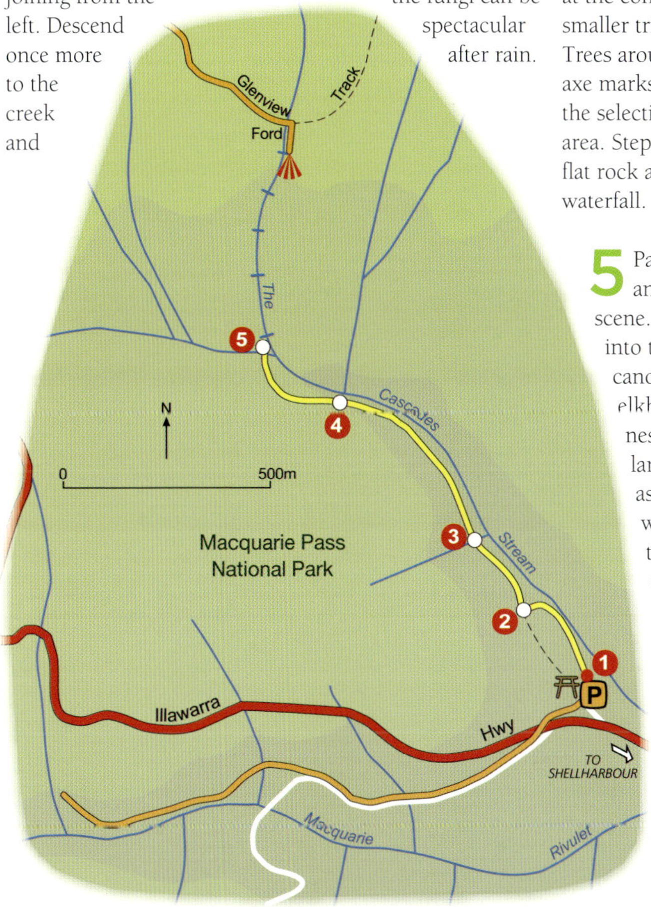

Giant stinging tree

4 You'll next reach the base of a railed ramp which rises up and then descends to creek level at the confluence with a smaller tributary creek. Trees around here bear axe marks, reminders of the selective logging in the area. Steps deposit you on flat rock at the base of the waterfall.

5 Pause here awhile and admire the scene. If you look up into the lush forest canopy you'll see elkhorns and birds nest ferns; these large epiphytes are associated more with subtropical than temperate rainforests. Retrace your steps to return to your car.

Out and about – Exploring nearby

The Cascade Walk ends at the lowest of several drops that the Cascades Stream makes as it tumbles downhill; higher up, the stream is forded by the Glenview Track, a broad, easy track open to walkers but now closed to vehicles (access is 3.3 km further up the highway). The start point for another walk can be found across the Illawarra Highway from where you have parked the car. A road servicing properties gives access to a minor footpath through the rainforest and along the lower reaches of Macquarie Rivulet (Walk 27 takes you to an upper level). The path rises and falls along the northern bank, negotiating exposed tree roots in places, to visit several delightful pools along the rivulet but then deteriorates. Return the same way.

Illawarra environment – A song in the forest

Along the length of the Escarpment, forested gullies offer a habitat for superb lyrebirds. Even if you don't see one of these large birds, scratching around the forest floor, you're quite likely to hear one. At first, you might think you're listening to a currawong or perhaps a whipbird, but then you realise that all these songs are coming from the same source: the lyrebird is the master of mimicry. A male arranges a range of bush sounds in a symphony that includes his own buzzing and clicking calls, in order to entice the females (who do sometimes sing themselves, but with less mimicry). When in full display, the male also throws his long tail feathers over his head and dances about on a mound of leaf litter that he has scraped together. It's an incredible performance, heard most often during the winter breeding season. Your best chance of getting tickets is at places where the lyrebirds are used to people, such as at Minnamurra Falls.

27 Waterfalls of Macquarie Rivulet

It may not be a fully-fledged river but Macquarie Rivulet certainly punches above its weight! As it plunges off the Illawarra Escarpment, its course through the Macquarie Pass National Park is punctuated by four named waterfalls and several unnamed ones, not to mention its many cascades. This delightful return walk, on an old road closed to traffic, takes you through open forest and rainforest to a regenerating farm and ruined farmstead and then on to easy-to-get-to Rainbow Falls and Mulangong Falls.

At a glance

Grade: Easy/medium (variations medium/hard)

Time: 2 hrs 30 mins

Distance: 7 km return

Conditions: Slippery rocks at rivulet crossing

Finding the track

Proceed as for Walk 26 but continue up Macquarie Pass for 2.4 kilometres, then turn left into signed Clover Hill Road and park by the locked gate.

Walk directions

1 Rounding the gate, descend gently on the Clover Hill Road management trail. Initial filtered views of the southern escarpment are soon lost as the road crosses the first of several creeks. A second creek crossing soon follows.

2 You'll presently be surrounded by the tall, moist forest typical of the park's creek gullies. Despite its height, much of the forest in the Macquarie Pass area is regenerating after many years of extensive logging. The track now undulates a little before contouring above another creek gully. Water usually flows in this more major creek which you cross on a concrete bridge as the track doubles back.

3 In another 400 metres or so, cross a branch of this creek and emerge from the moist forest into a large clearing, once part of Clover Hill Farm. A grove of tall cabbage tree palms stands stark against the unfolding view of undulating foothills and distant ocean. These venerable specimens must have been saved from the forest clearances.

4 Look for the detour right (about 200 metres on a grassy farm track) to inspect the ruins of the farmstead, built against a rock wall. Swamp wallabies keep the grass very well clipped, and quieter walkers may see them. Back on the main track, you soon reach a second clearing where all that remains is a benchless table. Cross a third and final clearing to reach a saddle.

5 Ignore the path that continues on into forest (see the variation) and hunt to its right for an overgrown path that looks less promising. As you prepare to push through low bracken you have a direct view of the imposing north-south escarpment. Macquarie Rivulet plunges over these cliffs as Macquarie Falls: after prolonged rain, Macquarie Falls and neighbouring McAndrew Falls should be visible from here. The track soon makes an easy descent and merges with a lower track from the left, reaching

Balancing Rock

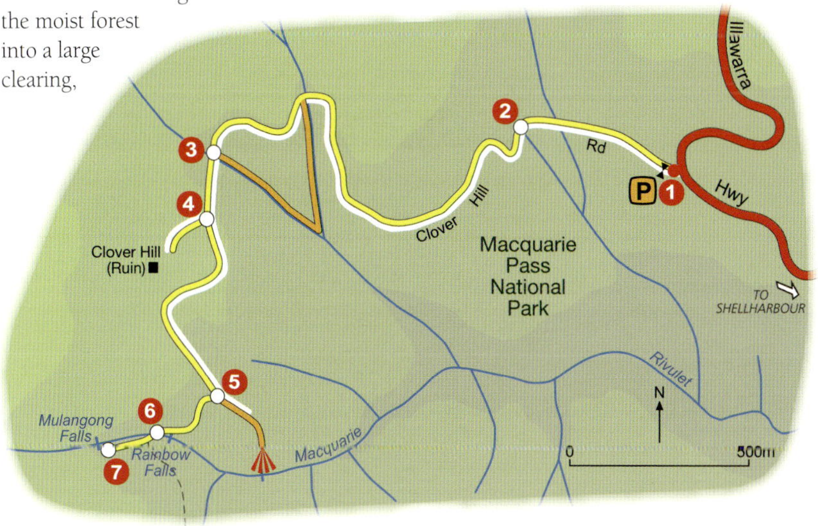

the bank of Macquarie Rivulet. Take care, as the smooth rock can be slippery.

6 A few metres downstream, Rainbow Falls plummets down a narrow defile. The sling around a tree at the top of the falls is a clue that summer canyoners abseil down this rivulet. A few metres upstream, a dilapidated concrete causeway can be used as a crossing point. From here the path divides: take the upstream footpad (right) but soon divert right on a minor footpad down to the creek. Here a huge balancing rock partly obscures your view of a beautiful set of cascades below Mulangong Falls. The base of these falls can be viewed more directly by following the main footpad a little further before again diverting right down to the rivulet.

7 Now you should be just above Balancing Rock. You can carefully walk barefoot up the creek to the plunge pool at the base of the falls but be warned, the water is bracing even in summer. Return to the causeway crossing and retrace your steps to the car.

Rainbow Falls

View from the goat track

Walk variations

These two short but worthwhile detours will add to the walk's adventure (and difficulty) quotient.

At **waypoint 5** you can take the other track, which soon peters out in an open turpentine forest. An onward 'goat track', possibly formed by abseilers getting out of the rivulet, descends a ridge very steeply to reach a rock promontory overlooking a beautiful double waterfall, not named on the map. Return the same way.

For a **rainforest immersion**, walk down the creek branch at waypoint 3. In less than half a kilometre it joins the main branch at a lovely little pool. Walk this branch upstream a similar distance to regain Clover Hill Road. On the way up, look for outcroppings of coal shale at a creek bend; there are ancient leaf fossils in the large shale boulders in the creek bed.

Carrington Falls

Jamberoo and above

The lush, rolling hills around Jamberoo have a long tale to tell. Before the arrival of Europeans, the rich volcanic soils supported a mantle of dense, close forest that offered the Aboriginal people abundant resources. The rainforest was a magnet for European timber-getters who carted out whole stands of huge red cedars. The foothills were then cleared for grazing and this district prides itself on being the cradle of dairy farming in Australia. This gentle landscape has much charm, but oh for a few rights-of-way, so walkers could appreciate it better!

The steep, upper slopes of the escarpment have been less affected and today the rainforest around the upper Minnamurra River is safeguarded and justly treasured. Barren Grounds - where a hanging swamp developed over sandstone and inhibited tree growth - was also no use to settlers, so the plateau remains a wealth of wildflowers and wildlife. And then there are the waterfalls that plunge off the escarpment: Minnamurra, Carrington and Belmore, which can only be appreciated on foot. There are walks of varying difficulty here and plenty of wild country to explore. You will, however, need a vehicle to access most of it, as the area is lightly populated.

28 Jamberoo village

Once the haunt of escapee convicts who made their fortune illegally cutting timber, the Jamberoo valley gained respectability in the late 1820s as a dairy farming settlement. Perhaps to prove the point, the people of Jamberoo built numerous substantial churches, each with its own graveyard. It doesn't take long to see the heritage sites in this neat little village, so this itinerary includes a stroll along a country lane to stretch your legs and take in the unfolding views.

At a glance

Grade: Easy

Time: 2 hrs 30 mins

Distance: 5.5 km circuit

Dogs: On leash

Getting there:

Bus: Kiama Coachlines 701/2 runs on weekdays from Kiama rail station to Jamberoo

Car: Coming down the Princes Hwy from the north, take the Illawarra Hwy, then Terry St/ Jamberoo Rd; from the south take the Jamberoo Rd exit near Kiama; park in Reid Park, off Churchill St

Walk directions

1 Start in pretty Reid Park, where there are various facilities including a swimming pool. Pick up the footpath that follows Hyams Creek, named after Michael Hyam who was granted a parcel of land and laid out a private village with convict labour. He named the area Sarah's Valley, but the name Jamberoo – derived from an Aboriginal word for 'track' – later replaced it. Cross the creek via the footbridge and make your way over the grass onto Churchill Street, then turn right and walk up the hill.

2 From the street, take a look at Jamberoo Public School, built from local sandstone and cedar in 1878. Children made up a large part of the settling families hereabouts but until this was built, schooling was gained at church or at Jerrara further east. Jamberoo's largest cemetery – with graves from the 1860s – is a detour left up Drualla Road, but there are plenty of others closer to hand. Next door to the school is the 1867 Church of the Resurrection. This Anglican church originally featured a shingle roof; the tower, with its crenellations and attractive doorway, were added later. Turn right to walk up Chapel Lane.

3 St Matthew's Roman Catholic church was built in 1879; this area drew many poor Irish migrants. Wander up behind it to the churchyard, where the graves of pioneer families bear the brunt of wind and weather. Return down the lane and turn right to cross the creek once more. On the corner is the Presbyterian church of St Stephen's, another built in the solid Norman style. This one, constructed in 1876, has a more fortified appearance

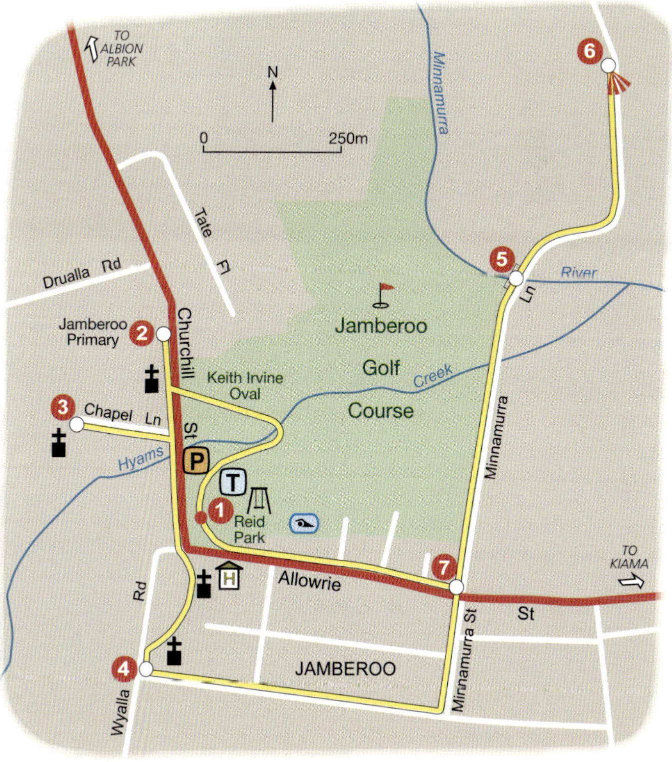

with rough-hewn stone and buttresses. Walk behind the church and through its small graveyard – note the grave of William Keevers, who was at the Battle of Waterloo – and wend uphill to a connecting graveyard.

4 The Gothic-style church, with a metal spire on a timber frame, was built for the Methodists in 1897. Unfortunately, the spire blew down a few months later and was never replaced, which accounts for the freestanding bell scaffold. Above the church, turn left to walk along Macquarie Street and then left downhill on Minnamurra Lane. Cross the main street and continue along this quiet, no-through lane.

This takes you past Jamberoo's attractive golf course, over Hyams Creek and then to the banks of Minnamurra River.

5 Upstream, the river plunges off the escarpment and down through national park rainforest (see Walk 29); here it burbles along at a more leisurely pace. All this would once have been dense, subtropical rainforest, thick with cabbage palms,

figs and liana vines. More recently this stretch of river was popular for picnics and swimming but sadly, there's no longer access along the banks, so continue on to round a bend and climb the stiff hill for improving vistas over the lush pasture.

6 Looking south, you can see the distinctive hump of Saddleback Mountain leading to Noorinan, a spur of the Barren Grounds plateau. Below you is *Minnamurra House*, dating from 1841 and one of the oldest houses in the Illawarra. Once regular transport was arranged to the port of Kiama, dairying became a profitable affair and the community thrived. The nation's first co-operative butter factory, opened in 1884, was located a short distance east. Now return along the lane to turn right into Allowrie Street.

7 There are several buildings of interest along here. The butcher's shop was the council chambers in the days when Jamberoo was its own municipality. Food for the soul can be found at Number Ten Arts Precinct; other appetites can be satisfied at any of the several cafés. You can't miss the Jamberoo Hotel, built in 1857 but renovated much later in Tudor style. Its shady garden is a pleasant spot to enjoy a refreshment, or you might prefer to picnic back in Reid Park.

Out and about – Illawarra Fly

Perched on top of the Escarpment above Jamberoo, the Tree Top Walk at the Illawarra Fly offers a very different perspective of the landscape. This 1.5-kilometre walk with interpretive signage includes a raised walkway with sections cantilevered over the rainforest canopy and leads to a 45-metre-high spiralling tower with panoramic views of forest, farmland and coast. The complex, which also includes a café and gift shop, is located on Knights Hill Road, via Jamberoo Mountain Road. Open from 0900 daily; entry fee; T 1300 362 881, or visit www.illawarrafly.com.au.

29 Minnamurra Rainforest

This is one walk that is as much about the journey as the destination. The upper reaches of the Minnamurra River are protected by Budderoo National Park and a lot of effort has been made by the NPWS to allow sustainable access to patches of delightful subtropical and warm temperate rainforest along its reaches. This walk combines the Loop Walk (a short circuit if you want to keep the walk easy) and the Falls Walk, a more strenuous uphill detour to view spectacular waterfalls and a slot gorge. Superb Lyrebirds - less guarded here - are often to be seen scratching through the leaf litter.

At a glance

Grade: Medium

Time: 1 hr 45 mins

Distance: 4.2 km circuit

Conditions: Shortcut option

Info: Open 0900-1700 daily; allow time to complete walk - last access at 1600

Disabled access: First 500 m is suitable for assisted wheelchairs

Getting there:

Bus: Kiama Coachlines 701/2 visits on weekdays from Kiama rail station

Car: North of Jamberoo, turn west onto Jamberoo Mountain Rd then right on Minnamurra Falls Rd to the end; vehicle entry fee applies

Walk directions

1 Start at the Visitor Centre, where you can discover more about the rainforest environment. Exit at the rear of the building to enter the rainforest. The rich, volcanic soil and the location of this gully, in a protected amphitheatre that catches moist warm breezes off the ocean, combine to support subtropical rainforest unusually far south. The elevated boardwalk soon crosses the Minnamurra River via a suspension bridge.

2 The canopy of the forest is dense with elkhorns and birds nest ferns, while the understorey includes tree ferns, ground ferns, rock orchids and moss. Water dragons often sun themselves on the riverbanks. Walk on, avoiding the large-leafed stinging tree. Just before the third bridge is a large red cedar: these were once abundant in the Jamberoo district but an uncontrolled trade in their timber during the early nineteenth century means that large specimens are now rare.

3 Off to the left of the path, with a bench seat at its base, is a towering strangler fig known, not surprisingly, as the Big Fig. Skirt the fern-filled gully and cross another suspension bridge: from now on you remain on the true left bank of the river. The path now starts to ascend and reaches a space where a treefall caused by a severe windstorm has breached the normally dense canopy, giving us a rare opportunity to see regrowth in a rainforest. Just beyond is the path junction with the Falls Track.

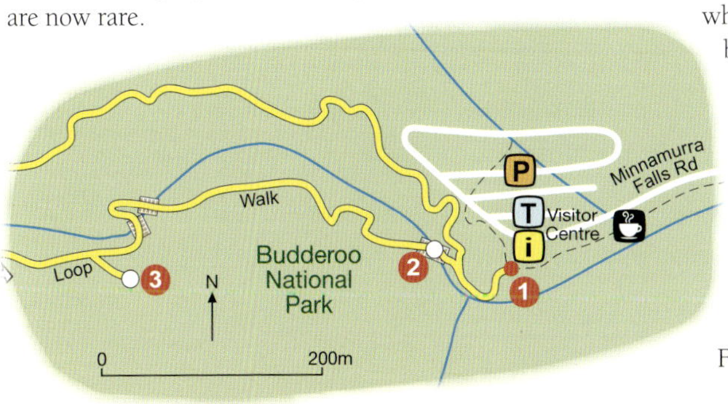

4 If you're short of time or breath, this is the spot to shorten the walk and continue downhill to the start. Otherwise, head uphill on the paved Falls Track. This return path climbs steadily through mixed eucalypt forest, frequented by lyrebirds. This section of path was built after a landslide in 1989 blocked the earlier route. Hard to believe, but this area was once used to graze cattle, which is why invasive weeds are a continuing problem here. The path levels somewhat to contour along the slope.

5 Pass left of Lyrebird Falls on a side stream. To your left, there are filtered views to be had down valley; in spring, the green canopy is punctuated by flowering Illawarra flame trees. Further along, at a path junction, turn left to a lookout platform above Lower Minnamurra Falls. The river pours into a slot gorge,

an ancient dyke formation created when an intrusion of lava later eroded. Return to the junction and head left to the spacious platform below the Upper Falls.

6 Here, water off the swampy Budderoo Plateau tumbles over ledges as Minnamurra Falls. Before you leave the deck, do look up to admire the birds nest ferns above. Now return down the steep slope. At the junction at

waypoint 3, keep left to follow the boardwalk steadily downhill. There are some thick woody vines along this section, well adapted to get from the forest floor to the light of the canopy.

A gate on the left serves as an exit if the Visitor Centre has closed for the day; before 4 pm you should continue back through the centre. A short distance further down the hill, you'll find the Lyrebird Café, BBQs and picnic tables.

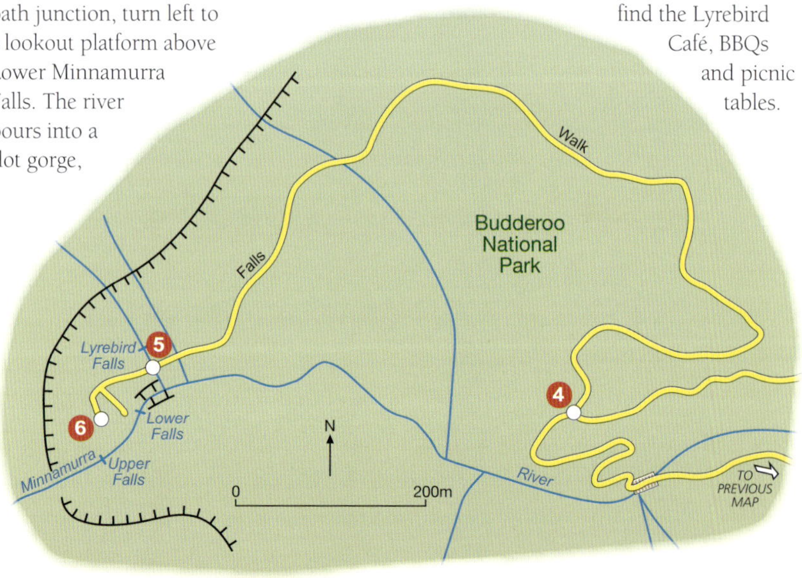

30 Illawarra Lookout

At Barren Grounds, the Illawarra Escarpment has eroded to create a spur that juts out from the main plateau. The shallow soil above sandstone drains slowly and supports a 'hanging swamp' or heath where trees tend to be stunted or are absent altogether. Wildflowers, however, thrive in these conditions and are rife in spring and early summer. If that isn't enough, this short and easy walk leads to a dramatic lookout over the coast and hinterland.

At a glance

Grade: Easy

Time: 1 hr

Distance: 2 km return

Conditions: Wildflowers in spring and summer

Finding the track

On the northern edge of Jamberoo, head west on Jamberoo Mountain Road to wind steeply uphill. Some 2.2 kilometres past the entrance to a Benedictine retreat, watch for a sharp left turn into the Barren Grounds Nature Reserve and park at the picnic area at the road end.

30 Illawarra Lookout

Walk directions

1 Once you've digested all the information in the picnic shelter, take the track by a low gate, signed to Illawarra Lookout. This is also the first section of the Griffiths Trail, featured in Walk 31, and it begins as a broad service trail.

2 The vegetation soon changes from open forest to high sedges and coral fern, typical of the heathland. The track passes between tea trees, low-growing wattles and old banksias, mottled ochre-red with lichen. There is usually something flowering along this stretch: look out for shrubs of swamp boronia, tea tree, whitebeard, peaflowers or delicate, freestanding yellow goodenia and lilac dampiera.

3 At the signed T-junction, go left for 100 metres on the narrower footpath to reach a railed lookout platform on the rim of the escarpment.

4 Here at the Illawarra Lookout, power lines plunge off the escarpment down to the farmland of the Jamberoo Valley. This

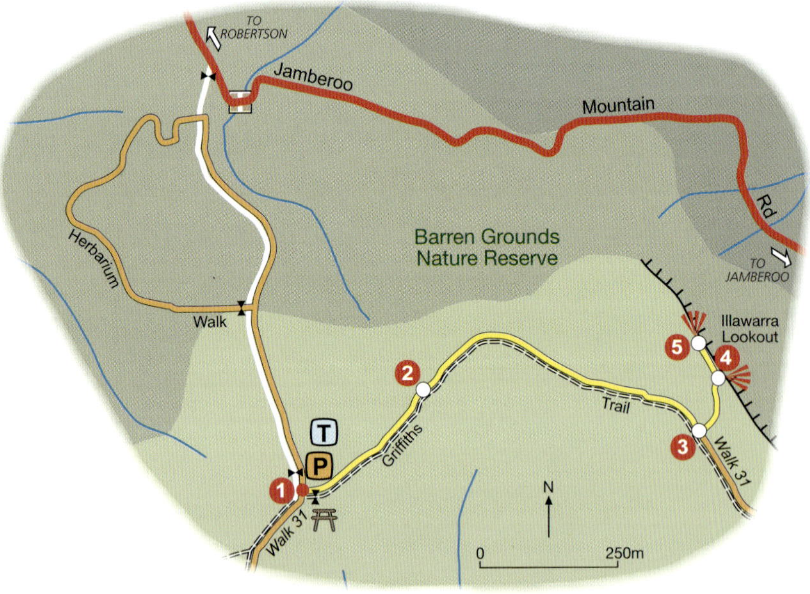

scarp receives a high level of rainfall and moisture-laden cloud off the coast, but if the view is clear it stretches far over the southern Illawarra, with Lake Illawarra, the chimneys of Port Kembla and the Five Islands beyond often visible.

5 Hidden around to the left is the site of the old lookout, which was enclosed with a low rock wall. There is a beautiful banksia nearby and more views along the escarpment to the northwest. Return by the same route.

Walk variation – a winter herbarium

Nearby, another short walk loops through a patch of heath that is especially interesting in winter. From the picnic area, walk down the road in the direction of the entrance for 750 metres or so (past a parking bay) to the Nature Study Centre. Behind this, you'll find a sign for the Herbarium Trail. The short path is punctuated by informative panels and wends for less than a kilometre through open heath and then taller heath of tea tree, banksias and dagger hakea that attracts honeyeaters when in flower. Tunnels in the dense undergrowth are a sign of long-nosed potoroos. There is also a boggy section where carnivorous plants thrive. When the path ends back at the road, turn right to walk the few hundred metres back to your car.

31 Griffiths Trail

This walk continues beyond the Illawarra Lookout to discover the wide range of plant communities that belie the name Barren Grounds. It's a surprisingly varied circuit around the plateau: along escarpment, through lush forest, over heath-covered ridges and across creek gullies. A highlight is the Stone Bridge, a very pleasant spot to enjoy a picnic or – if the creek water isn't too chill – a refreshing dip.

At a glance

Grade: Medium

Time: 3 hrs

Distance: 8 km circuit

Conditions: Wildflowers in spring and summer

Finding the track

Same as for Walk 30.

Walk directions

1 Take the footpath by a low gate, signed to Illawarra Lookout and Griffiths Trail. At a path junction, detour left for 100 metres to the viewing platform at Illawarra Lookout, offering sweeping views over Jamberoo Valley and out to the southern Illawarra coast.

2 Return to the junction and turn left to climb up over boggy stretches where patches of moss adorn sandstone and carnivorous sundews are scattered on the ground. Presently, the track enters high forest as it nears the cliffs; a brief detour to the edge allows you to look over the canopy of moist forest below the escarpment, with necklace heath clinging to cracks in the rock face.

3 Soon the path drops into The Glen – a lush gully filled with swordgrass, tree ferns and bracken – to cross a tributary of Lamonds Creek. As you climb out of the gully, the vegetation changes once more to open heath, with tussocky grass and sparse trees. Look for a minor footpad leading left onto a rocky outcrop, from where filtered views are to be had.

4 Soon after a four-way junction, among trees on the left, you'll find Saddleback Trig. Presumably it once offered a view of Saddleback Mountain to the east, along the route taken by the surveyor Robert Hoddle when he blazed a track from the Southern Highlands to Kiama in 1830. Back at the junction, take the path heading south, signed to Stone Bridge (although the

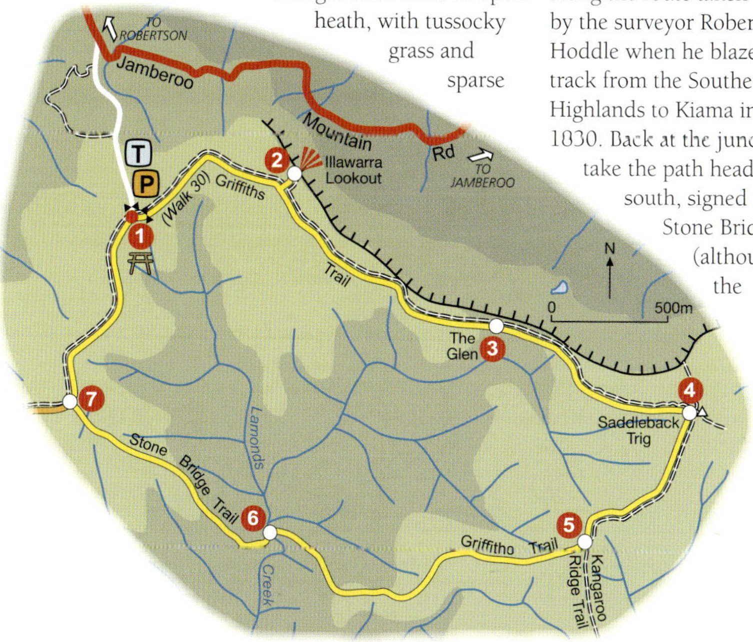

3 kilometre distance is a little generous). The path continues level, with views right to Knights Hill, through stunted heath plains vegetation, dotted with mallees. After 800 metres, you'll reach a Y-junction; left is signed to Kangaroo Ridge.

5 Take the right branch of the track and head downhill as the track becomes rockier and more eroded, passing through a cover of tall banksias. The track becomes wetter underfoot as it makes a steeper descent – punctuated by erosion-prevention humps – down to Lamonds Creek.

6 Draining off the organic-rich soil of the swamp, the acidic water has an increased power to dissolve the sandstone it flows over. Here it has formed a course under the rock, forming the natural Stone Bridge, and also a large deep pothole just downstream. There is also a swimming hole here, accessed by a low but slippery rock ledge. Cross the rocky ford and climb steps out of the gully then continue up on a rocky track between tea trees, wattles, banksias, and mallees. The ascent eases on broader, flat rock and, 1.2 kilometres from the creek, you reach a T-junction.

Illawarra environment – Flightless birds

About 180 different birds have been recorded feeding or nesting on Barren Grounds, but two residents are particularly special. The isolated plateau was dedicated as a reserve as early as 1956 to ensure the protection of the Ground Parrot and the Eastern Bristlebird. These two endangered species are semi-flightless: able to flutter a bit but that's the extent of it. The small bristlebird is well-camouflaged in dull brown with grey throat, but it does have a loud, harsh call (which sounds suspiciously like *pretty birdie*). The more striking ground parrot is a bright green, barred and spotted with yellow and black; it issues an ascending, bell-like call at dawn and dusk. Either might be flushed out from the edge of the heath as you walk down the track but if not, you'll just have to be content with the other 178 birds.

7 See the boxed text for a possible extension here; the Griffiths Trail, however, goes right. Follow the level, grassy track – kept well cropped by swamp wallabies – back through heath of dagger hakea and coral fern to arrive back at the picnic area.

Mt Broughton from Cooks Nose

Walk variation – Cooks Nose

Another point in the reserve is well worth visiting as an extension to this walk. At the junction at waypoint 7, head west and, after 400 metres, turn left and walk 2.2 kilometres along the undulating Cooks Nose Trail. This takes you to a fine viewpoint off the southern escarpment rim, from where you can see down the Brogers Creek valley to Mt Broughton, or the Wedding Cake as it is known locally. The path to the lookout undulates through scrub of banksia and hakea which both attract honeyeaters when in flower.

32 Carrington Falls: the south rim

At a glance

Grade: Easy

Time: 2 hrs

Distance: 5.5 km return

Conditions: Best after rain

Wheelchair access: To main lookout

The Kangaroo River hurtles 50 metres off the escarpment plateau as Carrington Falls, one of the most spectacular features of the southern Illawarra's hinterland. The area's scenic qualities were acknowledged back in 1887 by the Governor of New South Wales, Lord Carrington, who declared Carrington Falls a recreation reserve. It is blessed with a variety of walking opportunities, thanks to the long-term efforts of the local families who managed the reserve and built tracks, lookouts and picnic areas. The south rim of the gorge is the best place from which to view the falls, a particularly awesome sight when in full spate.

Finding the track

On the northern edge of Jamberoo, head west on Jamberoo Mountain Road for just over 18 kilometres, then turn left onto unsealed Carrington Falls Road. Follow this for 1.6 kilometres to a Y-junction; veer left and, in 800 metres, turn right (signed to Carrington Falls lookout) to soon reach Thomas Place.

Walk directions

The falls from below

1 Thomas Place picnic area is named after a long-time promoter of the Carrington Falls area, who acted as a guide and served on the Carrington Falls Trust. The picnic area has fireplaces, picnic tables, toilets and an information board. Take the path to the left of the paved wheelchair access path. It leads towards the south rim of the upper Kangaroo River gorge. At a T-junction, detour briefly left to reach the first of four lookouts on this loop, each one closer to Carrington Falls.

2 The view here is of the imposing north rim of the upper Kangaroo River gorge. The verdant farmland of Robertson slopes down towards the gorge in the distance. Back at the junction, keep ahead near the escarpment to soon merge with the disabled access path to reach the main lookout, with a clear view of the impressive waterfall. Beyond here, the path parallels the cliff line, descending and ascending an 80-metre length of steel-grated steps which negotiate a deep cleft in the cliff to soon reach two more lookouts.

3 Detour to each lookout for superb close-up views of Carrington Falls' sheer 50-metre drop, close enough to feel the spray when the Kangaroo River is really powering. The path now loops away from the flat rock platform that forms the lip of the falls (there is no formed access to the expanse of potholed river bedrock). Return through the forest to the paved path which you then follow back to the picnic area. Left (south) of the loop

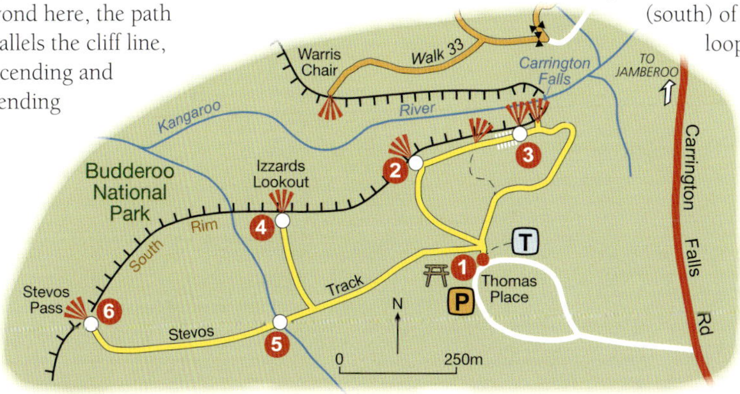

track, find the signed start of Stevos Track and walk through dry forest for 360 metres to a signed track junction; detour right for 200 metres.

4 From Izzards Lookout, the views stretch down the gorge to distant farmland as well as across the gorge to the cliffs of the northern rim. Back at the junction, head right, continuing on Stevos Track; Stevo and Izzard were two locals who opened up this route to the farmland down valley. The broad management trail is presently blocked by bollards; the onward path passes a large termite

mound before descending to cross a small creek.

5 Across the creek, the path narrows and presently veers towards the scarp, providing filtered glimpses of the valley. It appears to end abruptly in the middle of nowhere with a sign directing you back to Thomas Place. It does continue on, however, and as it begins a slight descent you can see the former logging road has been cut in to the slope. Until the 1940s, bullock teams hauled timber out of the steep valleys on such roads, to be processed at the Missingham sawmill at Carrington Falls. At one point you must divert above (right of) the cutting, which has been made impassable by treefall; if you find yourself doubling back, you've gone wrong. Reach a 'Stevos Track' sign and beyond this, an information sign warning you of the dangers of continuing down into the valley.

6 A rocky outcrop, left of the track, is a good spot to enjoy the filtered valley view before your 2-kilometre return to Thomas Place. The old road – known on old maps as Missingham Pass – zigzags its way further down into the gorge but it becomes progressively more difficult to follow and peters out, providing Kangaroo River access only for experienced bush navigators.

Illawarra environment – Retreating gorges

The hinterland of the southern Illawarra is blessed with a swag of dramatic waterfalls - Carrington, Belmore, Gerringong, Minnamurra and Macquarie (not to mention Fitzroy Falls, featured in a companion book). These falls all form the head of spectacular, deep gorges, cut by the creeks and rivers that flow off the sandstone plateaux. The depth of these gorges seems out of all proportion to the often modest water flow, but it does not require a torrent to erode this rock: seepage through sandstone cracks can bring down large blocks at a time. These waterfalls are all about 90 kilometres upstream of the coast and it's been estimated that the gorges have been cutting back at the rate of about 3 kilometres every million years. On average, that's 3 millimetres a year, so don't loiter too long on the edge!

33 Carrington Falls: Nellies Glen and the north rim

At a glance

Grade: Easy/medium; variation: medium/hard

Time: 2 hrs

Distance: 5 km return

Conditions: Optional creek scramble should be avoided in wet conditions

The Carrington Falls area is such a fabulous spot that it takes two walks to do it justice! Of course, this walk exploring the gorge's northern rim can be easily connected to Walk 32 for a longer excursion. There's plenty of variety on offer here with a series of fine lookouts, a couple of swimming holes (one with its own waterfall), a ferny dell, and a cascading creek to explore. A short but challenging extension on an early-nineteenth-century path allows you to immerse yourself in a lush rainforest gully.

Finding the track

As for Walk 32, but leave Carrington Falls Road right after 1.4 kilometres to park at the Carrington Falls camping and day-use area.

33 Carrington Falls: Nellies Glen and the north rim

Walk directions

1 The low-key camping area is a vestige of the days before Carrington Falls was incorporated into Budderoo National Park. Despite its status as a well-kept secret, it has recently been upgraded with composting toilets, fireplaces and a picnic shelter. Take the signed walking track beyond the shelter but soon detour left for a short distance on a footpad.

2 This leads to the languid Blue Pool, filled by a feeder creek that forms Nellies Glen further downstream. The creek is drained by one of the many heathland swamps on Budderoo Plateau and always seems to flow. Back on the main track, soon ford the stream (you may get wet shoes here) and negotiate any muddy patches. After 600 metres on the track, you reach a signed junction.

3 Head right for the Missingham Lookouts, 1.5 kilometres away. You soon emerge from the eucalypts as the track skirts a farm boundary to your right. It becomes rockier and eroded, dropping and curving to ford a minor stream on stepping stones. After a short uphill pinch back to the fence line, the track swings right at the corner of a paddock, then left through tall forest and away from the farmland. Turn left at a junction to walk 100 metres to Missingham East Lookout.

4 Carrington Falls is tucked out of sight behind the gorge's northern rim but there's a superb view down valley and of both cliff lines. The dark green rainforest vegetation is a clear feature of the sheltered gullies below. Return to the junction and bear left.

5 At another junction, head left to very soon reach Missingham West Lookout where the view is similar, though there are now glimpses of the Kangaroo River almost 300 metres below. Look left

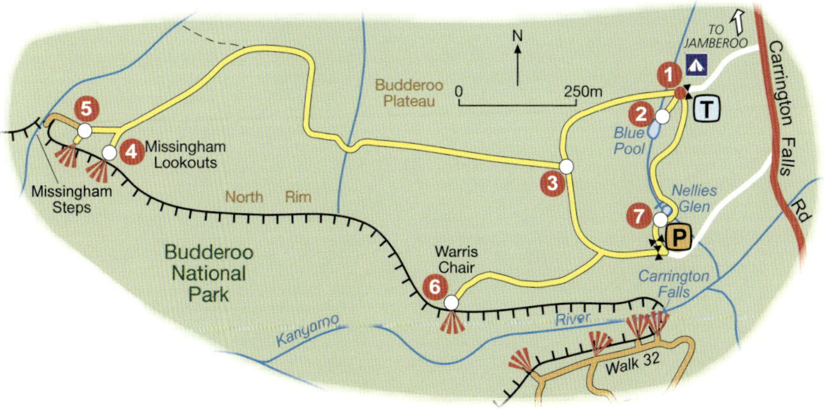

to see the strangely eroded anvil-shape rock forming an outlying part of the near cliff line. Return to the junction at waypoint 3 and veer right, following the track signed to Nellies Glen and Warris Chair. At the next junction head right again: this narrower path soon parallels the escarpment closely, with filtered views of the opposite sandstone rim.

6 Whoever Lady Warris was, her chair is a beautiful piece of natural sandstone furniture which beckons you to sit and soak in the spectacular valley-and-scarp vista. The falls are still obscured but if you stand at the lookout railing you can see a cascade and plunge pool below the main drop. Back at the junction, head right and soon reach a barrier and lay-by at the end of a dirt road. Just to the left is the short path through another barrier to the Nellies Glen picnic area.

7 Nellies Glen – just 50 metres further on – is a delightful, ferny glade downstream of Blue Pool where this walk commenced. On a warm day, the deep pool, fringed by water gums, makes an idyllic swimming hole. It's refreshed by the modest waterfall pouring off a sandstone ledge. The large boulders enclosing the pool downstream must have been moved there long ago by a stupendous flood. The creek appears to have changed course below the pool: a low undercut rock wall replete with mosses and small ferns no longer serves as its main channel. It's a fascinating place to explore.

Out and about – camping at Carrington Falls

Free drive-in campsites in a natural bush setting are a rarity in national parks close to Sydney and Wollongong so why not spend the night camping at Carrington Falls? With swimming in warm weather, wildflowers in spring and early summer, and plenty of nearby walks on offer year-round, it has a great deal to tempt lovers of the great outdoors. Many of the walks in this section are a short drive from here. It is only a small camping area so it's probably best to avoid holiday weekends and summer holidays if you crave solitude.

The quickest (and most scenic!) return is to scramble right of the waterfall and rock-hop upstream to pick up a footpad on the true left bank of the stream. In dry conditions, you can remain in the rocky creek bed most of the way – there are several more cascades to observe – before exiting right onto an unsigned track that returns to the camping ground. If the scramble isn't to your liking, return via the road or else along the track you took earlier.

Walk variation – Missingham Steps

In the early 1900s, John Missingham had his timber workers use their holidays to construct a track off the escarpment down into a steep side-creek gorge as a way of getting down to Kangaroo River for the Sunday recreation of his workers' families. Those were the days! The track's name comes from the steps that were hewn from the rocks, some of which are still intact. This track is no longer maintained or promoted by NPWS but confident rock scramblers who want a taste of the lush rainforest environment beneath the cliffs can access the route from waypoint 5. The onward track passes a signboard outlining the dangers of proceeding. The path deteriorates and ends near rocks where the way ahead involves a scramble down a cleft: steep but not exposed. You are now in a rainforest world where little light penetrates. It's possible to descend Missingham Steps Creek; rocks in the creek bed are slippery even if the creek isn't flowing and the best route will probably be marked by a combination of pink tape, paint and metal tags on trees. You can get a good feel for the gorge without going too far. Only experienced navigators with plenty of time should contemplate descending all the way to the river.

34 Belmore Falls

In the southern Illawarra, the escarpment is no longer a straight line facing the coast; here it turns inland and becomes pleated, with finger-like ridges. Between each finger, a waterfall plunges off the cliffline. This short walk offers views of one such – Belmore Falls – both from afar and close up. In times past, a path led to the base of the falls but this is no longer maintained.

At a glance

Grade: Easy
Time: 30 mins
Distance: 1 km circuit
Conditions: Best after rain

Finding the track

Drive to Robertson via Jamberoo Mountain Road/Illawarra Highway. Turn left on Meryla Street to cross the railway line, right on South Street, and left onto Belmore Falls Road. After 7.8 kilometres, turn left onto a one-way loop road (signed to Hindmarsh Lookout) to the first car park.

34 Belmore Falls

Walk directions

1 Beyond the bollards of the parking area, follow a walker totem past some picnic tables and downhill through dry woodland dominated by stunted silvertop ash. The understorey here features broad-leaf geebungs, tea trees, wattles, hakea, drumsticks and honeyflowers. Just to the left is the first of four viewpoints.

2 Hindmarsh Lookout is named after an early settler who owned land nearby (see Walk 35). It offers a view straight down the valley of Barrengarry Creek to its confluence with the Kangaroo River beside the village of Kangaroo Valley. Return a short way and pick up the path along the fenceline to a second, unnamed viewpoint, also looking down valley. Continue alongside the railing.

3 Belmore Falls Lookout delivers, as promised, a direct view across to the amphitheatre where Barrengarry Creek makes a tiered fall, with a large pool between the two drops. Rainforest flourishes in the gorge below, which is often lapped by a sea of mist and temperatures are less extreme than up on the plateau. The falls were named after the Earl of Belmore, Governor of NSW from 1868-72, who spent his summers at nearby *Throsby Park*. Further along, yet another lookout gives a slightly closer view of the falls.

4 From here, you can see more closely into the amphitheatre, cut into hard Hawkesbury Sandstone. To the right of the top waterfall is a large cavern undercutting the cliff face; over time, water seeping down joints and along natural weaknesses must have loosened a huge slab of sandstone to create this. Now retrace your steps to waypoint 3 and the climb the steps to the loop road.

5 The footpath continues on the other side, passing picnic tables and toilets, or you can simply turn right and walk down the road to return to your car. If you arrived at the Falls from the east, it is worth walking or driving further along Belmore Falls Road to the ford over Barrengarry Creek. There is a good view back to the falls from the cliffs just beyond the ford but you should take care near the edges.

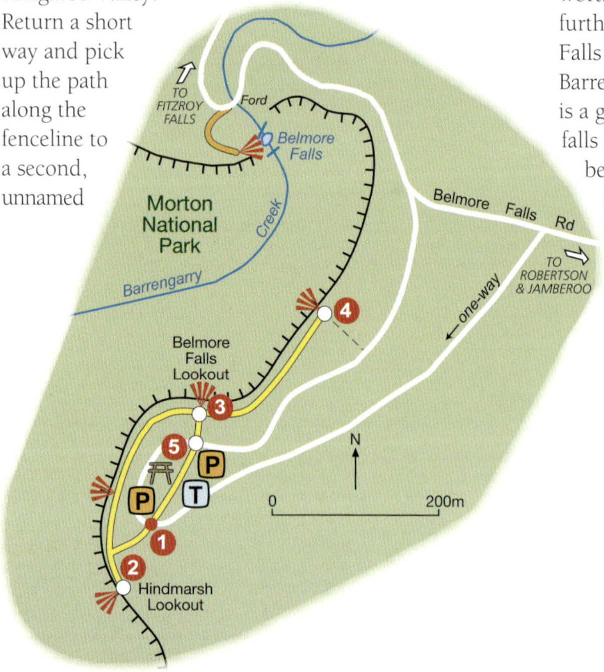

Out and about – other nearby falls

Fitzroy Falls, plunging 81 metres over sheer cliff, are easily visited. From Belmore Falls, continue along Belmore Falls Road, turn left into Myra Vale Road, then right onto Nowra Road (the road linking Kangaroo Valley and Moss Vale) to soon reach the Fitzroy Falls turnoff (park use fee applies). Here, you'll find an excellent NPWS Visitor Centre and the Falls Café, plus two well-marked paths. The first - along the West Rim - is the one that most visitors take to view the main falls, with Lady Hordern Falls below and nearby Twin Falls. The East Rim Walk is longer, features more wildflowers and a ferny gully, and offers good views down the Yarrunga Valley as well as across to Fitzroy Falls. Both these walks are described in detail in *Best Bush, Coast and Village Walks of the Shoalhaven*, another book in this series.

Gerringong Falls are a little further off the beaten track. Drive 2.8 kilometres west of the Barren Grounds entrance on Jamberoo Mountain Road and turn west (left) on Budderoo Track to soon park by the locked gate. Continue on foot for almost 4 kilometres and then turn right on a footpath across the heath to the escarpment rim where Gerringong Creek makes its leap. Return the same way. The walk is a total of 15 kilometres return. Alternatively, jump on a mountain bike and cycle the Budderoo Track and the Hersery Fire Trail (a right turn 6.2 kilometres from the locked gate), then walk the final 400 metres to the falls.

Gerringong Falls

Fitzroy Falls

35 Hindmarsh Ridge

Hindmarsh Ridge juts out above Kangaroo Valley to its north, forming the watershed between the gorges of Barrengarry Creek and Kangaroo River. The ridge, formerly Yarrawa State Forest, is now part of Budderoo National Park and its old logging roads provide access to a series of superb Kangaroo Valley viewpoints. This is not an area frequented much by walkers so you're very unlikely to encounter anyone all day as you amble through dry forest that is typical of the escarpment.

At a glance

Grade: Medium

Time: 4 hrs 30 mins

Distance: 12.5 km return

Conditions: No signage; unfenced lookouts

Finding the track

Drive to Robertson via Jamberoo Mountain Road/Illawarra Highway. Turn left on Meryla Street to cross the rail line, right on South Street, and left onto Belmore Falls Road. After 6.7 kilometres, turn left onto Wallaby Hill Road. Keep straight ahead – you may need to open and close a farm gate – to park near a locked gate at the road end.

Walk directions

1 Round the gate marking the boundary of Budderoo National Park and walk along the Yarrawa Track. After 250 metres, fork left on a broad logging track which becomes steeper and includes anti-erosion humps as the escarpment is approached. The maintained track ends abruptly, but a short easterly scrub-bash to your left brings you to a rocky bluff on the cliff edge.

2 Here is your first fine view: a prospect of the farmland and forest of the upper Kangaroo River and Gerringong Creek valleys, separated by a steep spur off Budderoo Plateau. Back at the track end, it's possible to breach the escarpment by following the onward course of an old logging road through McAndrews Gap, one of several named passes off Hindmarsh Ridge. Trending right, the route continues above the left side of a gully head and swings down left below the cliff line, in places obviously once cut-in as a track. It hugs the cliff base as it descends; take great care near the edges! Part way down, someone has discreetly placed a cairn. A good place to stop is when you get a view of the 85-metre cliff line to the left.

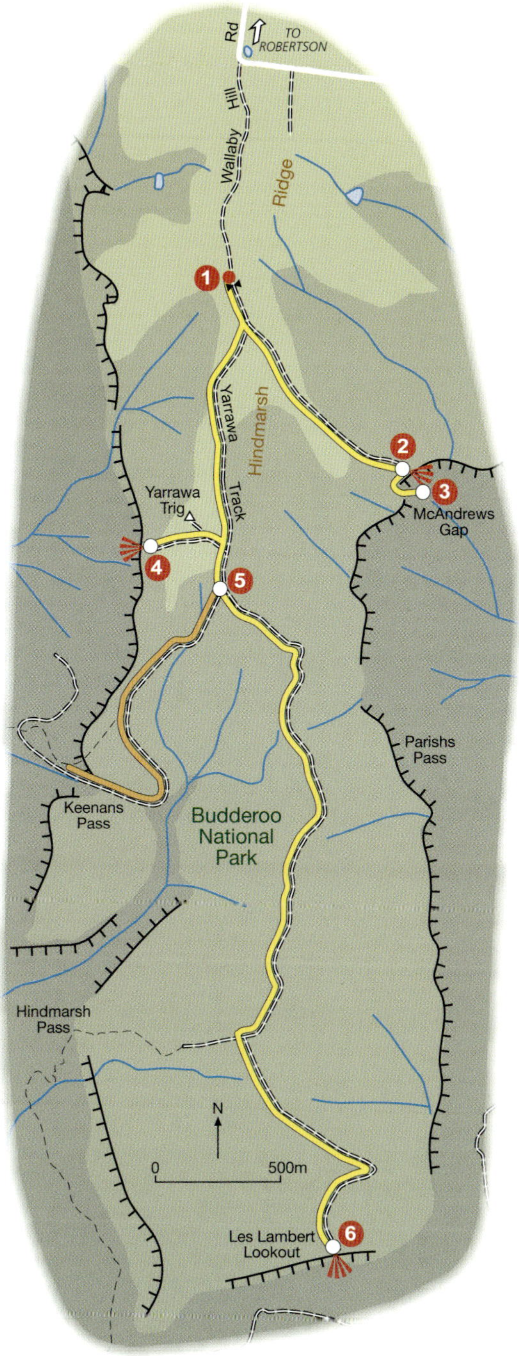

3 Return the same way to the track end and head left, back on the Yarrawa Track, continuing south for a kilometre. At a local highpoint (there may be a small cairn) look closely for a sandy path leaving right amid heathland shrubs. The path soon broadens to an old vehicular track and in some 350 metres you should arrive at the plateau's western edge.

4 The vista here atop the 100-metre high cliffs is compelling. Below are the rainforested slopes of Barrengarry Creek gorge which, several kilometres upstream, is headed by Belmore Falls (seen more closely on Walk 34). Downstream, the view widens to include Kangaroo Valley farmland and beyond the volcano-like Mount Scanzi stands prominent. Return to the main track; trig-baggers could try detouring left for nearby Yarrawa Trig en route but the side track becomes something of a scrub-bash. Continue south along the main track to where it soon forks.

5 Take the left branch for a bit of a trudge over mostly level ground. At one point, a large patch of carnivorous sundews has colonised a poorly-drained forest clearing. About 2.2 kilometres from the last junction you reach another track fork. Head left on an unmapped former logging track which has subsequently been bulldozed further along, presumably as access for fighting fire. Ignore a left branch, negotiate a little tree fall and you'll reach some low rocks where the track peters out.

6 Clambering up these rocks, you'll find yourself on the ridge's southern escarpment. The map declares this to be Les Lambert Lookout and – we'll go out on a limb here – this is the best of all views of Kangaroo Valley. It is all the better for its obscurity. To your left is Budderoo Plateau's southern promontory, then the Cambewarra Range stretches across with Bugong Gap separating Mount Scanzi to the right. Laid out below this backdrop is the full extent of Kangaroo Valley. To your right, a steep forested spur drops down to the distinctive outlier: Binya Hill. Linger for lunch or a rest on the eroded sandstone furniture before making your way back to the walk's start point.

Walk variation - Keenans Pass

Two other passes off the cliff line can be visited on this walk - Hindmarsh Pass and Keenans Pass. The latter is definitely worth visiting for the contrasting rainforest that thrives below the plateau. Take the right track branch at waypoint 5. The track descends and after 500 metres or so it begins to swing left. You can divert here on a footpad out to the escarpment for more Barrengarry Creek gorge views. The track continues to descend into tall moist forest, passing left of a low cliff line and soon follows above a deepening creek gully. A huge sandstone boulder has landed on the road, having cleaved from the cliff face above and shattered a swathe of forest on its way down. This might mark the turnaround; further down the road a gate marks the boundary between the national park and private property.

The Blowhole

Around Kiama

Kiama is a pretty seaside resort town, set among green, rolling hills. However, all this serenity hides a turbulent past: the geology of this area points to volcanic activity around 260 million years ago. Walkers can see ample evidence of this as they hug the splendid coastline from Minnamurra Headland to Gerringong. Signs of the region's heritage are well preserved in the settlements of Gerringong and Kiama, while those who want a bit more solitude can head inland on a historic route to Saddleback Mountain. The South Coast rail line runs through the centre of the town and Kiama Coachlines (T 4232 3466; www.kiamacoachlines.com.au) operates a bus service that links Kiama to Jamberoo and Gerroa.

Kiama from Saddleback Mountain

36 Kiama: a walk back in time

The centre of Kiama offers walkers a wealth of historic features and natural delights. The town first developed as a port for local timber getters and dairy farmers, but it thrived in the late 1800s when a trade in quarried basalt or blue metal was established. As a result its heritage is a fascinating mix of maritime, agricultural and mining stories. All that, and it has the Blowhole too!

At a glance

Grade: Easy

Time: 2 hrs

Distance: 3.5 km circuit

Dogs: Permitted on leash

Getting there:

Train: Kiama rail station

Car: Town parking; pick up the walk anywhere along the circuit

36 Kiama: a walk back in time

Walk directions

1 In Railway Parade, you'll find the Family History Centre, one of the most complete genealogical centres in Australia. Cross Terralong Street, Kiama's main shopping strip, to reach the Scots Presbyterian Church, dedicated in 1863. The compensation for land later claimed by the railway paid for the addition of its fine steeple. Across Shoalhaven Street is the Old Fire Station, now a community arts centre, and you then reach Hindmarsh Park, named after Michael Hindmarsh who was one of Kiama's first landholders.

2 On the corner of the park is a memorial arch built shortly after the First World War. Walk up Collins Street, passing the quaint cottages built in 1886 to house the families of quarry workers. Today these unique weatherboard terraces are home to a variety of gift shops and cafés.

3 At the top of the terraces, pick up the lane that runs along the rail line and follow it back downhill. Beyond the railway towers is the solid bluestone building that was once Kiama's public school. Walk under the railway and cross the street to Black Beach Reserve. The explorer George Bass anchored his whaleboat in this sheltered bay in December 1797 and, from the 1830s, timber and dairy produce was regularly shipped on steamers to Sydney from here. A detour left along a path takes you below Pheasant Point to a rock swimming pool, originally for ladies only.

4 Return and follow the sea wall around, passing a plaque commemorating lives lost when the *SS Bombo*, transporting blue metal, sank in 1949. A detour up a flight of steps allows you to inspect a survey obelisk, from which distances in the area have been measured since 1861. Continue around to a wooden jetty.

5 There are usually pelicans loitering here. If not, you can certainly see Kiama's sculpture to commemorate a pelican that died after ingesting discarded plastic bags. Nearby is Robertson Basin, which took 16 years to excavate and was opened in 1876 to provide safe harbour for the growing number of trading ships. By 1883, some 400 tonnes of rock were leaving daily, much of it destined for roads, rail and tram lines in Sydney. Further around the point is the gentlemen's rockpool, now open to all. From here, walk up the steps and follow the

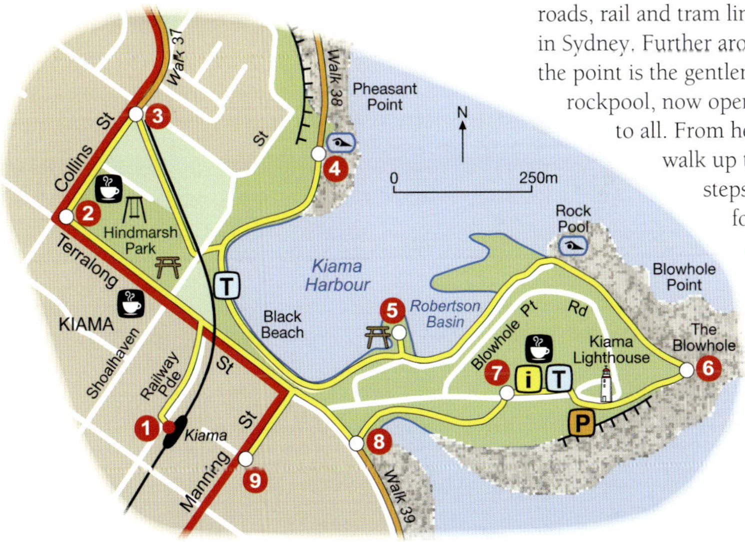

footpath to several viewing platforms for Kiama's signature, the Blowhole.

6 This natural feature is likely the source of the town's name: the Wodi Wodi name *Kiarama*-a means 'where the sea makes a noise'. Less romantically, it is a vented volcanic dyke under the latite-basalt platform; a helpful nearby sign explains the dynamics. While there is usually some level of activity, the blowhole really gets going when the seas run from the southeast, at which times its water plume can reach a height of 60 metres, with a whoomp sound to match. Once you've torn yourself away, circle the attractive lighthouse nearby. It was opened in 1887 with an oil-fuelled lamp to guide boats into the harbour. Now head over to the buildings beyond this.

7 Here you'll find a kiosk and a well-stocked visitor centre with friendly staff. Next door is the beautifully restored Pilot's Cottage, run by volunteers of the

Illawarra environment – Kiama's dry-stone walls

If you're a serious dairy farmer, you don't want your prize Illawarra shorthorns wandering off, and this is where Kiama's dairying and quarrying heritage overlap. On the downs around town are some 400 heritage-listed dry-stone walls, many constructed over a century ago. The main crafter of dry-stone walls – whereby stones are fitted together without mortar – was Thomas Newing, who built walls for over sixty years. Walkers can enjoy examples of Newing's work on the Bushbank Mill Track, which starts at a lay-by on the Princes Highway heading south of Kiama, a kilometre before the Mt Pleasant Lookout. The path follows the route of the Old Coast Road and visits the ruins of an 1856 steam mill used to grind wheat into flour. The tradition continues; there is still an artisan building dry-stone walls in the area today.

local historical society as a maritime and regional museum (open Fri-Mon 1100-1500). Walk along the grassy southern edge of the point to enjoy a view over Storm Bay before crossing Terralong Street.

8 Nearby is the whitewashed Christ Church, built in 1859. If you get a look inside, you'll see its ceiling, installed in 1872, resembles the inverted hull of boat. In the small graveyard behind the church is the resting place of John Gowan (1763-1837), a corporal of marines who arrived on the Sirius, the flagship of the First Fleet. Follow Terralong Street back to the town centre but turn left on a detour up Manning Street to admire some venerable, well-preserved buildings.

9 The Bank of Sydney built two of these in the prosperous 1880s; a figurehead of its beady-eyed chairman at the time adorns the facade of one. The town hall across the road is a relative newcomer, at a mere hundred years old. Walk around the startlingly pink Italianate post office, completed in 1889, and continue up Terralong Street, pausing to admire the less ostentatious 1860 courthouse, one of the oldest buildings on the South Coast. Walk under the iron rail bridge; until this was built in 1892, the railway only reached as far as North Kiama (or Bombo) and travellers had to be ferried by horse-drawn carriages to the centre of town. This brings you back to near your start point, and to a cluster of cafés.

37 Spring Creek

The valley of Spring Creek has seen many changes. The creek that drains off Saddleback Mountain provided Aboriginal people with fresh water until European settlers cleared the gully for dairying. A Chinese family had a market garden here around 1900. When surrounding farms were subdivided for housing, the area was considered too flood-prone and the local council was persuaded to rehabilitate the wetlands. Today, it protects a diversity of ecologies and is rich in birdlife. This short walk also visits the neighbouring cemetery and could be combined with an excursion out onto Bombo headland.

At a glance

Grade: Easy

Time: 1 hr

Distance: 3 km one-way

Getting there:

Train: Kiama rail station; check timetable for a return from Bombo station

37 Spring Creek

Walk directions

1 Walk down Railway Parade and turn left into Terralong Street. Cross the corner of Hindmarsh Park and stroll along the historic terrace cottages in Collins Street. This climbs to become Gipps Street, which veers left, high above the southern end of Bombo Beach.

2 On the downhill, turn right into Hothersal Street to reach an underpass under the Princes Highway. This skirts Charmian Clift Reserve, named after the writer who was born in Kiama, and brings you to the northern bank of Spring Creek.

3 Make the short diversion north to visit Kiama cemetery, where many of Kiama's early settlers are buried, including a cedar getter named David Smith who was the first to build a residence in 1832. Also here is the grave of

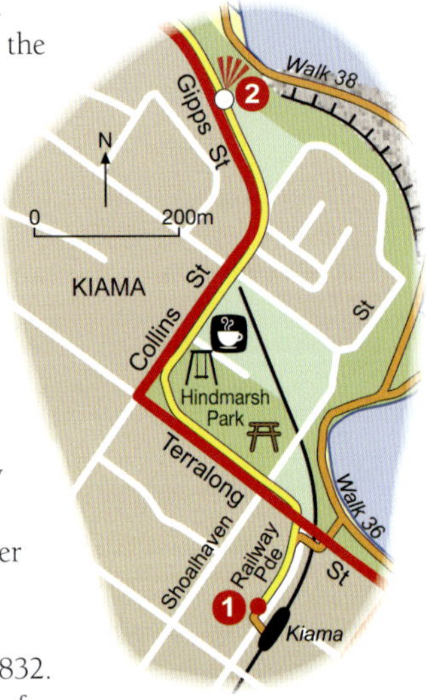

Illawarra environment – Green and golden bell frogs

This green and gold Aussie battler was once very common along coastal NSW but has become endangered due to the spread of a fungal disease and loss of habitat. It needs still or sluggish water, ideally with rushes or reeds, and a varying water level. The adult frog is between 5 and 10 cm long and while its colouring can vary, all have a creamy strip on each side that runs over its ear and along the body. They often bask in the sun, perched on reeds or on other objects, and have a distinct call as if growling. Spring Creek hosts one of the forty or so key populations remaining in NSW.

Thomas Newing, who was responsible for building many of the dry-stone walls around Kiama. On the hill above the cemetery is Robert East Reserve, from where you can gain a fine view over the Bombo headland.

4 Return to Riddell Street, the lane that runs along the edge of the cemetery and fork left to enter Spring Creek Reserve. A paved footpath leads you through remnant rainforest – where numerous new plantings have been made – and along the northern bank of a brackish lagoon. From here you have a view across to coral trees, where cattle egret often roost. A section of boardwalk carries you over swampy ground where she-oak and sedges thrive. After passing an exit to Glenbrook Drive, you reach another junction with a sign to the bird hide.

5 Keep left to cross the small dam wall and follow a path along the spit between the lagoon and the freshwater lake. This ends at the elaborate observation hide, strategically placed among rushes and reeds (although the rushes can be a little obtrusive). This lake attracts many wading birds such as egrets, herons, ibis, spoonbills and swamphens, as well as migratory birds. Smaller birds such as wrens and fantails also frequent this area.

6 Return to waypoint 5, and turn left to continue through the parkland, passing some old lemon trees. Keep left on a cycleway to cross Spring Creek once more and then Willow Creek. An information board provides plenty of detail on life in the reserve. From here you have a choice. One option is to exit nearby on Jamberoo Road (noting the 1870 bluestone culvert) and turn left to follow hilly Terralong Street to Kiama's centre, a walk of less than 2 kilometres. Alternatively you could retrace your

steps to waypoint 3 and either continue on foot to Kiama or catch a train back from nearby Bombo station. If you time to spare, see Walk 38 for a diversion to Bombo Headland.

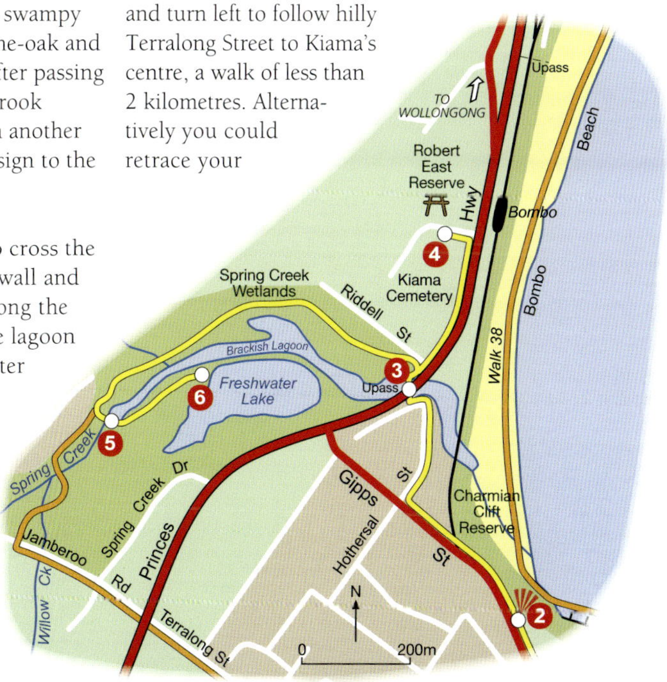

38 Kiama Coast Walk: Minnamurra to Kiama

It is now possible to make a continuous walk of the stunning coast line all the way from Minnamurra to Gerringong, thanks to a newly opened stretch of the Kiama Coast Walk. The whole walk can be done in a long day but we've broken it into two more leisurely sections to and from Kiama (see walk 39), making use of the convenient train service. Kiama's plentiful overnight accommodation options allow for a superb weekend of walking. The way from Minnamurra to Kiama takes in the picturesque Minnamurra estuary and headland, dramatic Cathedral Rock and the moonscape of Bombo Headland's abandoned quarry.

At a glance

Grade: Easy/Medium

Time: 4 hrs

Distance: 11 km one-way

Conditions: Tide options at the Boneyard and Pheasant Point

Dogs: On leash and may need to stay on cycle/walkway behind beaches

Getting there:

Train: Start and finish linked by rail: from Kiama rail station, catch a northbound train to Minnamurra station

38 Kiama Coast Walk: Minnamurra to Kiama

Walk directions

1 From Minnamurra station (east side) head along North Street to North St Reserve where there are toilets and water. It's worth detouring left here, following the Minnamurra River upstream through parkland as far as desired for the tranquil riverside views. The river (or rivulet) has had a short journey to the sea, plummeting over the Illawarra Escarpment as Minnamurra Falls west of Jamberoo. A sea wall backing private property prevents progress downstream from the reserve.

2 Walk south along Charles Avenue, passing Rangoon Reserve and soon turn left into John Oates Reserve and pick up the footpath around Minnamurra Point - this is the start of the official Kiama Coast Walk. Follow its blue totems through the parkland close to the river mouth. Make a short detour on a footpad out to the point for closer views of Rangoon (also called Stack) Island, named for the sailing ship which foundered on rocks on a stormy night in 1870, fortunately without loss of life. North is the Minnamurra sand spit and the coastline of Killalea. While here, note the headland's columnar basalt rocks, a feature of the north Kiama coastline.

3 Clamber around the rocks to soon reach the northern end of Jones (or Boyds) Beach. Lifeguards patrol this beach in summer so it's a good swimming option. Walk the beach and detour briefly around rocks for a close, sea-level view of aptly named Cathedral Rocks, with Bombo Headland beyond. The spires of rock are comprised of volcanic latite, sculpted by millennia of erosion along jointlines.

4 Return to the sand and take the southernmost set of steps up to the strip of reserve behind the houses of Cliff Drive. Walk between the backyards and the cliff edge, mainly on grass, to reach a picnic table where the reserve broadens; turn right to reach Cliff Drive. Take the shared foot/bike path left through a locked gate and soon veer left off the sealed path, descending to a wooden boardwalk backing the Boneyard, a tiny beach and cove which is a popular picnic and snorkelling spot. There was once a large jetty here from which blue metal was transported from quarry to ship.

5 If the tide is right (if it isn't, go back to the main path), you can clamber around the rock shelf to the northern point of Bombo Headland and scramble up some easy rock blocks to the top and a mown grassy path where you head left. Soon veer left again, still on a grassy path to a lookdown over the old, fenced Boneyard basalt quarry. It's a sheer drop to the quarry and a sign warns of the danger of proceeding. The quarry's columns frame the view of

the southern part of Bombo Headland, Bombo Beach and beyond to Kiama lighthouse.

6 Retrace your steps and keep veering left as other paths merge from the right. You will soon be following right of a fence preventing a fall into the quarry. Meet up with the bike path you left earlier and soon go left down a lane for close-up views of the bizarre basalt columns, which have served as a backdrop on film and television. Continue on a gravel track, leaving it left after it loops, to walk over rock to below the southern part of the Bombo Headland outcrop.

7 A deeply incised gully stops further progress below the headland cliffs so you must retrace your steps a short way to rejoin the gravel track and then walk to the parkland reserve at the northern end of Bombo Beach. Those with an enthusiasm for birdlife should consider a different route from here, joining Walk 37 on a visit to Spring Creek. At high tide all walkers might need to follow the road under the railway and turn left to follow the route of Walk 37 into Kiama.

8 If the tide permits, descend a concrete path and walk south on Bombo Beach, continuing below Pheasant Point on a rock platform: the plum colour of the rock here is striking. Soon you reach Kiama rock baths (ladies only in olden times) where a swim comes with a great view of Blowhole Point.

9 Continue around Kiama Harbour, first on a concrete path and then on a wider concourse behind Black Beach. This is the closest point to Kiama rail station, reached by climbing steps to Terralong Street (where you might linger for a coffee), walking right under the railway bridge and turning left into Railway Parade and up the hill to the station.

Illawarra environment – Gerringong volcanics

There's something strange about the rocks you walk over and past in the southern Illawarra. Many of them issued forth from an offshore volcano southeast of Kiama in the Permian period, some 260 million years ago. Lava flows cooled into latite, a hard rock akin to basalt, which faulted as distinctive hexagonal columns exposed in the quarries at Bombo. Tiny particles of volcanic debris also fell into a shallow sea and settled to become reddish tuff or sandstone, the sediment covering marine organisms and preserving them as fossils. Volcanic activity occurred over a long period, so there are layers of latite and sandstone plus intrusions and dykes, where molten rock has oozed through fissures in existing rocks. Over the millennia, the mineral-rich rocks have eroded into the fertile soil that encouraged the area's early dairy trade.

39 Kiama Coast Walk: Kiama to Gerringong

This second day of the Kiama Coast Walk (see Walk 38) boasts not one but two blowholes, a handful of lovely beaches, rock platforms, and kilometres of elevated, rolling farmland edged with precipitous cliffs. This all makes for an exciting day's walking surprisingly close to civilisation. The new coast-hugging track between Loves Bay and Werri Lagoon forms the heart of this walk. With luck, its popularity might encourage plans for a similar path over the headland south of Gerringong Harbour, making it feasible to walk the coast all the way to the Shoalhaven River!

At a glance

Grade: Medium

Time: 5-6 hrs

Distance: 17 km one-way

Conditions: Exposed to sun and wind

Dogs: On-leash only and not allowed on some beaches

Getting there:

Train: Kiama rail station; finish at Gerringong station

Car: Park at Gerringong station and catch a northbound train to Kiama station

39 Kiama Coast Walk: Kiama to Gerringong

Walk directions

1 From Kiama station's north side, walk down Railway Parade and cross Terralong Street to reach Black Beach. Walk along the path to the man-made boat harbour, frequented by pelicans. Pass right of the fish market to soon reach a swimming pool, once for gentlemen bathers only. Head around Blowhole Point on the grass, keeping left of the loop road, to reach the lookout platforms above the famous Kiama Blowhole, a spectacular sight and sound when a big south-east swell is up.

2 After an obligatory pause to capture a waterspout or three on camera, take in the nearby lighthouse, the Visitors Centre and perhaps the Pilots Cottage historical museum. Then take the concrete footpath under the big Norfolk pines and walk around Storm Bay. Head around Church Point between the rocks and Kiama's Showground, and descend to Kiama Surf Beach (patrolled during the swimming season).

3 Pick up the concrete path at the southern end of the beach, ascending to a grassy reserve at Kendalls Point. Now descend some zig-zag steps, left of a holiday park, to Kendalls Beach. From the southern end, ascend to a blue totem and follow the path to Kaleula Head where a seat allows for a relaxed study of the coastline.

4 *Kiama Coast Walk* totems direct you to Gwinganna Avenue and then left into Boanyo Avenue (diverting you around the sea-grotto of Friars Cave) and, after a short road walk south, to turn left down a gated lane. This brings you to the water's edge, just a short

distance from the Little Blowhole, which is at its best in a northeast swell.

5 From Little Blowhole Reserve, a path continues up around Marsden Head, on a grassy swathe, before descending via some steps to Easts Beach, set in a deep, picturesque cove. Climb the steps at the south end and go through a swing gate to enter a 'dog off-leash' park. Follow the blue totems around the edge of some old paddocks near the rocky coastline to surmount a dry-stone wall on a ladder stile. Now scramble around the rocks (or use a higher path) to the stony beach of Loves Bay and walk to a signboard at its southern end.

6 This marks the start of the previously 'missing link' stretch of the Kiama Coast Walk, opened in 2009. For the next 5 kilometres, you follow a broad dirt track on a fenced easement between private farmland and the cliff line. There are distance posts every kilometre as well as a series of information boards highlighting the local history and geology: one explains a long trench or dyke visible in the rock platform below.

7 Where the path skirts close to the railway, there is a break in the cliff line and an easy detour is possible to visit Boulder Beach, a pleasant spot for a rest. After the 3-kilometre sign, leave the path left (taking care!) to the cliff edge to view a distinctive rock stack off Bare Bluff.

8 From here it's a couple more kilometres of view-filled, undulating walking to reach Werri Lagoon which is rarely open to the sea. The elevation on this stretch of track makes for ideal whale-watching during the seasonal migration; see the box for tips.

9 Head along Werri Beach (or behind it) to the southern end; there is a sea-filled pool on the rock platform. To the right of the toilets is a grassy track that climbs the headland reserve east of Gerringong.

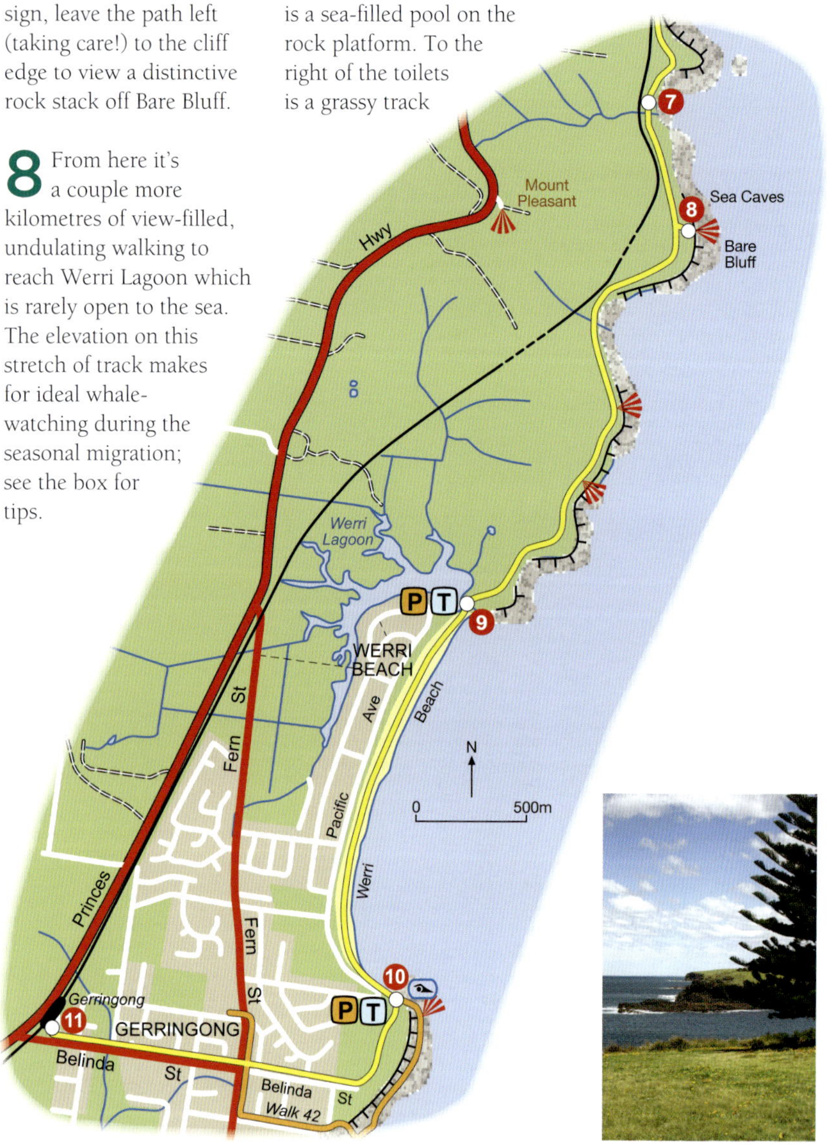

Walk variation

A much shorter walk from Kiama Heights to Werri Beach or to Gerringong can be made with the aid of the Kiama Coachlines bus that occasionally plies the backstreets between Gerringong and Kiama (weekdays only).

10 Follow this, passing a whale-viewing platform, to reach the end of Belinda Street at the top of Gerringong Cemetery. Follow Belinda Street west for 1.4 kilometres to reach Gerringong station, diverting right into Fern Street if you want to visit Gerringong's shops and cafés.

11 Gerringong's tiny rail station, built alongside a dairy co-operative to carry produce, is the furthest inland you have been on the whole walk. Return to your car or catch a train home.

Illawarra environment – Whale watching

In recent years Humpback whales have come back from the brink of extinction and can be spotted in large numbers along Australia's east coast on their annual migration between their Antarctic feeding grounds and tropical breeding grounds. They travel north in June and early July but tend to linger and frolic closer to shore when heading south with their newborn calves in October and November. Elevated headlands and cliffs make the best vantage points for land-based whale watching: you can scan a greater distance and whales often pass close inshore here. Pick a clear, calm day – the middle of the day is best as there will be less glare bouncing off the water – and watch for plumes of water. Humpbacks are spectacular breachers and also engage in fluke- and flipper-slapping and spyhopping, raising their heads vertically from the water. The less ostentatious Southern Right whale also passes through these waters.

40 Bonaira Garden circuit

This short walk in southern Kiama (or Kiama Heights) has great variety: a native garden, two tucked-away beaches, views in all directions and even a blowhole. A small amount of road-walking is required to link these features, but it's along quiet back streets and gives you the opportunity to check out the local real estate along the way.

At a glance

Grade: Easy

Time: 2 hrs

Distance: 5.5 kms circuit

Dogs: Permitted except on beaches

Getting there:

Train: Kiama rail station is a kilometre north

Car: From Kiama post office, follow Manning Rd south, turn left into Farmer St, right into Bourroul St and left to park at the end of Chapman St

Walk directions

1 From the end of Chapman Street, walk down the broad cycle/walking path. The path skirts the back of Kendalls Beach, passing neat-as-a-pin holiday cabins. After crossing Kendalls Creek, the path emerges at Bonaira Street. Cross this and cut across a corner of the playing field to then walk along a row of attractive fig trees and pick up the cycle path once more.

2 Bonaira Native Gardens, which you enter via a gate, is a work-in-progress tended by local bushcare volunteers. The path follows the creek upstream through remnant rainforest including cabbage tree palms and figs. On the right, a small plaque remembers the Wadi Wadi (or Wodi Wodi) people as the original inhabitants of the area. On a nearby slope in open parkland is an example of the drystone walling for which Kiama is famous. The path winds uphill to exit on Reid Street.

3 Turn left and, at the end, right into Mark Street. Before the railway line, turn left and follow it south to where the road curves and becomes Ocean Street. Whilst admiring the view inland, you might want to pick a bunch of wild fennel from the embankment here! Walk downhill on Ocean Street and, just before the entrance to Easts Beach Holiday Park, keep straight ahead on a grassy path that climbs the bank by a coral tree.

4 This easement gives public access to Marsden Reserve, though at times the grass can get a little high. A short way along, a footpath cuts back right downhill to a long flight of railed steps, leading down to Easts Beach, well worth the detour as long as your dog isn't with you, if only for the sumptuous amenities located at the back of the beach, mid-way between cabins.

5 Pretty Easts Beach, set at the back of a deep cove, is not accessible by car. At the far end, Munna Munnora Creek empties into the ocean. Make your

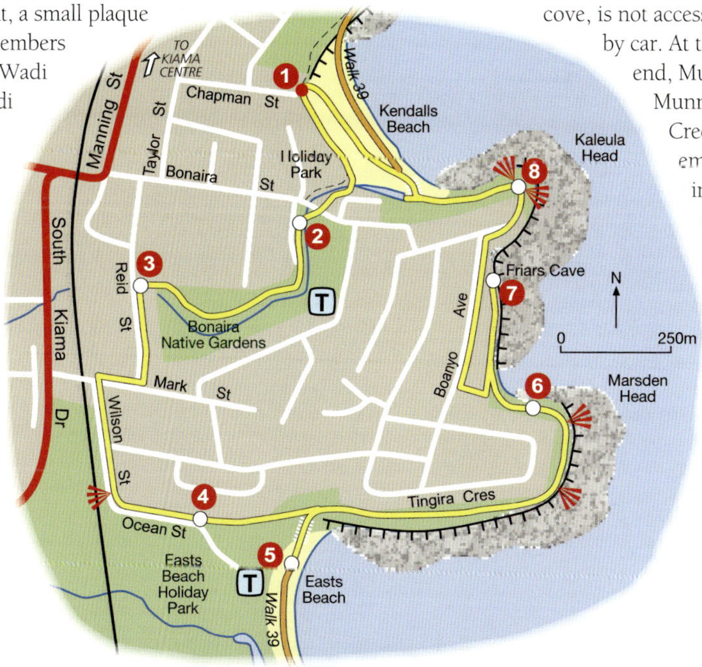

way back up the steps and continue along the reserve, pausing to look at Saddleback Mountain rearing up inland. A seat at the end of Marsden Head allows a comfortable view of the finger-like bluffs south; the recently opened path that wends over them continues to Gerringong (see Walk 39). Further around the head, a short footpad detours right to some volcanic latite that has cooled into columns. In the next bay, you reach a railed platform.

6 This is where the Little Blowhole – Kiama's lesser-known but more reliable blowhole – does its thing. It is at its noisiest and most spectacular when the waves are coming from the northeast. A short way

further along the footpath, a bench on a raised terrace is a good spot from which to view continued spurts. From here you can detour further around to view Friars Cave by crossing a rocky gully and continuing until fences and lantana thickets block your progress.

7 Friars Cave is another of Kiama's geological phenomena: the sea cave is said to extend some 700 metres inland. Return to the path and follow a lane (used to access water utilities) to exit onto Boanyo Avenue by a Coastal Walk sign. If you're in need of refreshments, the popular Little Blowhole Café is just around the corner at 4 Tingira Crescent. Otherwise, turn right and then right again into Gwinganna Avenue. At the end, a blue totem encourages you down an easement to reach Kaleula Head, from where you can see north to Blowhole Point and beyond to distant Bass Point.

8 Around the headland, another blue totem marks your footpath. Where it forks, keep high to walk through a patch of wind-shorn vegetation and then descend on steps to Kendalls Beach. From here, it's a short stroll along the beach and up the path to regain your start point.

41 Hoddle's Track and Saddleback

In the 1830s, surveyor Robert Hoddle hacked a route from the Southern Highlands to Kiama Harbour, making use of the high ridge and saddle connecting Saddleback Mountain and the promontory of Noorinan Mountain. This walk from the foothills of Foxground up to what remains of Hoddle's Track takes in a delightful combination of rolling farmland, heath and the largest sub-tropical rainforest remnant in southern NSW. The views along the way and from both landmarks are truly impressive.

At a glance

Grade: Medium

Time: 3-4 hrs

Distance: 9.5 km return

Ascent/descent: 450 m / 450 m

Conditions: Hoddle's Track is steep and eroded in places; take care near unfenced cliffs

Finding the track

From the Princes Highway south of Kiama, turn north onto Foxground Road. Follow this for 5.4 kilometres; the final kilometre is unsealed and winds steeply through rainforest. Park at the roadside opposite Hoddles Road and near the entrance to *Caruso*. If you are able to leave a second vehicle at Saddleback lookout, the walk can be shortened to 6 kilometres.

Walk directions

1 Walk up Hoddles Road, crossing over a cattle grid. This public right-of-way provides access to several farming properties. Continue steadily uphill through farmland before swinging right (north) where pasture gives way to tree ferns and rainforest on the left. The gradient eases and you go through an open gate.

2 The now unsealed farm trail climbs in fits and starts, leaving the rainforest for more pasture dotted with large boulders, long fallen from the cliffs of Noorinan Mountain. Pass to the left of a picturesque dam with a small jetty; nearby, a rusty old utility vehicle makes a great photographic subject.

3 Before leaving farmland for more rainforest pause to enjoy the views: up to the Barren Grounds escarpment, out to Seven Mile Beach and over rolling farmland to Coolangatta Mountain. The track becomes more eroded as it forges steeply uphill here. You'll soon reach a T-junction; a sign shows this to be Hoddle's Track which begins on Saddleback Mountain.

4 Head left, past a crumbling dry-stone wall, and soon emerge from the canopy to a splendid view northeast to Lake Illawarra and Port Kembla's industrial coastline beyond Jamberoo and the Minnamurra scarp. The track keeps to the grassy centre of the narrow saddle and occasional green-painted posts mark the way. Head through a stile, passing a sign indicating there's no track onto Barren Grounds Nature Reserve. The path steepens again as you approach the bluff of Noorinan Mountain.

5 Now the path levels and skirts left, hugging the mountain's southern cliff base through some delightful rainforest of liana vines and coachwood, a haunt for lyrebirds. In places you can discern that the path was once a formed road or cart track. As you climb once more there are a few fallen trees to negotiate before arriving at an amphitheatre below sheer, high cliffs.

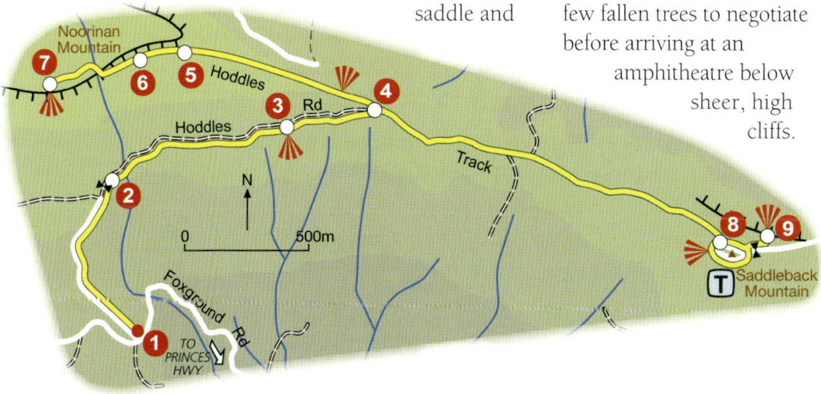

6 If you pause here to look up, you'll see one particular rock in the shape of a ship's prow appears to have a smooth knob of rock bolted to it. The path narrows as you cross above a creek gully to access the pass up right onto the edge of Noorinan Mountain. Take care as the scrubby footpad now swings left following near the cliff edge. After a few hundred metres through a heath of banksias, hakea and grass trees, you emerge at a rock platform with beautiful sea views over Foxground and to Saddleback Mountain.

7 Return the same way down to the *Hoddle's Track* sign on the saddle (waypoint 4) and continue ahead towards Saddleback. Round a gate, reach another *Hoddle's Track* sign, pass a fire trail on your left and descend quite steeply through more rainforest to yet another track sign. Walking under power lines, you now have a direct view of the telecommunications towers atop Saddleback. The track makes a gentler, grassy descent before the start of a 700-metre long haul steeply uphill. After a barrier gate, the gradient lessens and in a few hundred metres you're on the summit near the towers.

8 Nearby are a picnic table, toilets and a viewing platform providing views to Noorinan and glimpses of Coolangatta Mountain and the coast. Walk along the sealed loop

path, over a barrier gate and a short way down the access road; opposite a lay-by is a footpath left to the main Saddleback lookout.

9 The views from here are dramatic and there's an orientation sign so you can identify all the landmarks. It's said that on a perfect day, Kurnell's oil refinery and the sandhills of Cronulla can be seen. Directly below is a pocket of the subtropical rainforest – the Illawarra Brush – that once covered the entire area. Just beyond are the Jamberoo foothills, the cradle of dairy farming in Australia. Unless you've left a second vehicle at the Saddleback car park, return to Foxground via Hoddle's Track and Hoddles Road.

Illawarra history – Breaching the escarpment

Just as the Blue Mountains were a barrier to early settlement west of Sydney, so the Illawarra Escarpment proved an obstacle to trade further south. Valuable produce had to be transported long, slow distances overland to Sydney rather than by ship from a nearer South Coast port. So it was, in the winter of 1830, that Robert Hoddle was sent to survey a track from highlands to sea. Starting from the Wingecarribee Swamp near present-day Bowral, he had a team of twenty convicts – 'all but six the most idle and useless set of men' – cutting their way through almost impenetrable scrub and rainforest, to breach the escarpment at Noorinan Mountain and follow the narrow ridge to Saddleback Mountain. The present Saddleback Mountain Road follows the route of Hoddle's Track as it descended to Kiama's harbour. Despite the effort, this section of Hoddle's Track wasn't used for long before a more suitable route was found off the escarpment.

42 A Gerringong stroll

Gerringong's name is thought to come from Aboriginal words meaning 'fearful place', bestowed after sighting the arrival of Cook's Endeavour. Europeans certainly arrived in numbers around 1810 when cedar getters started clearing the hills, making way for farmers to grow grain on the fertile land, and then to graze dairy cattle. Permanent settlement, underway in the 1830s, suffered a setback when fire destroyed most of the commercial centre in 1872, but today Gerringong is a thriving coastal village. While it sits atop hilly terrain, walkers here are rewarded for their efforts with views in all directions.

At a glance

Grade: Easy

Time: 2 hrs

Distance: 3.7 km circuit

Conditions: Low tide needed for rock platform

Getting there:

Train: Gerringong rail station is a km west, along Belinda St

Car: Park near the corner of Fern St and Blackwood St, noting any time limits

Walk directions

1 If it's a weekend, you might want to start or finish your walk with a visit to Gerringong's Heritage Museum in Blackwood Street (open 1300-1600 weekends; modest entry fee) to view its interesting collection of artefacts from local properties. The simple stone church on the corner was built in 1874 to replace an earlier one burnt in the Great Fire. Across Fern Street at No.89 is the old police station, built two years later with 22-inch-thick walls. Start the walk from the corner of Fern and Blackwood Streets. Head south, passing the relatively young Town Hall and an even more modern playground.

2 Turn left into Belinda Street, lined with pine trees, to shortly gain a good view back inland. This pleasant avenue brings you to Gerringong's cemetery, whose inhabitants have an enviable position overlooking Boat Harbour. The oldest recorded grave belongs to Evan Campbell, who arrived with his family in the district in 1838.

3 After wandering among its headstones, walk north through parkland to read, on a plaque, the story of Lone Pine and, a short way further on at a viewing platform, about identifying passing whales. Continue along a broad track over the grassy hillside – popular with dog-walkers – as you take in the sweep of Noorinan Mountain, Saddleback and Mount Pleasant Ridge as they roll down to the sea. North across Geering Bay, you can see Red Cliff and a sea-stack just off Bare Bluff.

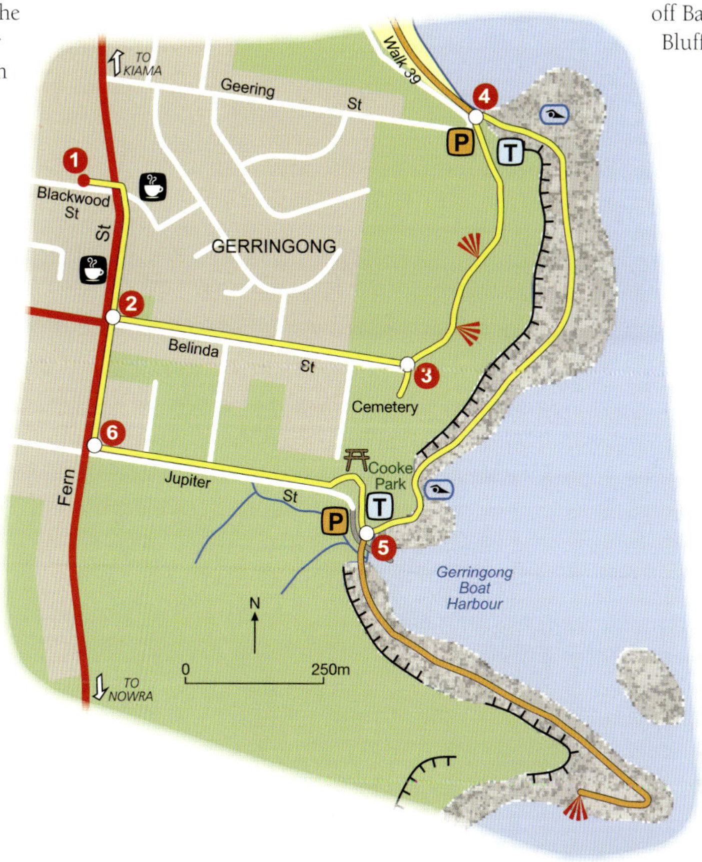

42 A Gerringong stroll

The holiday settlement behind Werri Beach stands on swampland reclaimed by early settlers. The track curves downhill by a re-generated green patch and reaches a road end.

4 This end of Werri Beach is patrolled in season. Alternatively, you might take a dip in the nearby sea-filled pool. Beyond this are signs of pre-history: the rock platform ahead is primarily basaltic lava from volcanoes active some 260 million years ago. Providing the tide permits, you can easily walk around the headland. The rocks underfoot become more varied as you near another swimming pool, backed by a concrete stand.

5 You have reached Boat Harbour, from where ships departed for Sydney in the late nineteenth century, loaded first with timber and, later, with butter from a co-op formed in 1883. A jetty that allowed cargo to be loaded directly onto large ships was destroyed by a storm not long before the Illawarra railway reached Gerringong in 1893, ending the village's reliance on shipping. Walk through Cooke Park, where there is a picnic shelter, and climb the steps to the left of the toilet block to reach picnic tables on a grassy

slope below the cemetery. Keep left to cross a gully of tangled remnant rainforest, then turn right and walk up Jupiter Street.

6 When you reach the junction with Fern Street you'll see, up on the left, the 1882 Catholic church, St Mary's Star of the Sea. The corner house on your right was erected in the early 1860s and served as the Boat Harbour Store. Turn right and walk past a series of attractive cottages and some not-so-attractive commercial buildings. Keep straight ahead, perhaps pausing for sustenance at the bakery or at the cosy vegetarian café nearby, to return to your starting point.

Walk variation

If you enjoy a bit of rock-hopping, a rewarding extension to the walk can be made from Boat Harbour at waypoint 5. Walk past the anchors raised from the harbour bed and hop down onto the rocky shore to pass an old channel cut into the rock. The headland cliffs reveal a layer of red tuff sandstone, formed as particles of volcanic debris fell into a shallow sea. Here it has weathered in interesting shapes and bears numerous fossils. A rocky cove around the corner is only negotiable at low tide when the sea is calm but it's worth making your way out onto the spit to look at the dramatic coastline south to Gerroa's Black Head (see Walk 43).

43 Black Head and Gerroa

The extensive rock platform below Gerroa's Black Head is a fascinating destination and not just for its beautiful rock pools. The site is on the Register of the National Estate with one of the best displays of fossils from the Permian period on the coast. Look for brachiopods, bivalves and the like on the platform's northern side where they are particularly abundant and where vertical dykes can be found in the cliffs. Don't tarry too long though, as remote Walker's Beach should only be approached near low tide.

At a glance

Grade: Easy/Medium

Time: 2 hrs 30 mins – 3 hrs

Distance: 8.3 km return

Conditions: Start walk on the ebb tide; high tide return alternative

Getting there:

Bus: Kiama Coachlines operates a service between Gerringong (rail connection) and Gerroa

Car: At Gerroa, leave Crooked River Rd east onto Riverleigh Ave; turn sharp right onto Park Rd and park at Emery Park

Walk directions

1 Emery Park has river views, BBQs, picnic tables, a gazebo and toilets. From the park, walk on the north side of Crooked River, on a narrow grass strip towards the sea. Pass a footbridge crossing the river mouth (it gives access to the Seven Mile Beach walk variation). Reach the eastern (Gerroa) end of Little Beach where, unusually, a boat ramp offers direct ocean access.

2 Head towards the rocks, flanked by a low cliff line, and continue southeast for about a kilometre over the shore platform to Black Head. The platform is a fascinating place, with exposed volcanic tuff rich in fossils, and weathers to create miniature rock pools. There are excellent views along Seven Mile Beach and inland to the escarpment west of Berry. These are even better seen from Black Head Reserve; you will possibly visit this on the return route but you can detour there now via a footpad by a few old fence posts.

3 Head north on the rock platform for a kilometre towards tiny Shelly Beach, which is more a rocky cove than a beach. Along this stretch, look out for fossils of marine life and, near the beach, a few pools that contain brightly coloured sea stars. Continue along the shoreline and, at the next, unnamed headland, you'll notice narrow vertical quartz seams in the cliff face.

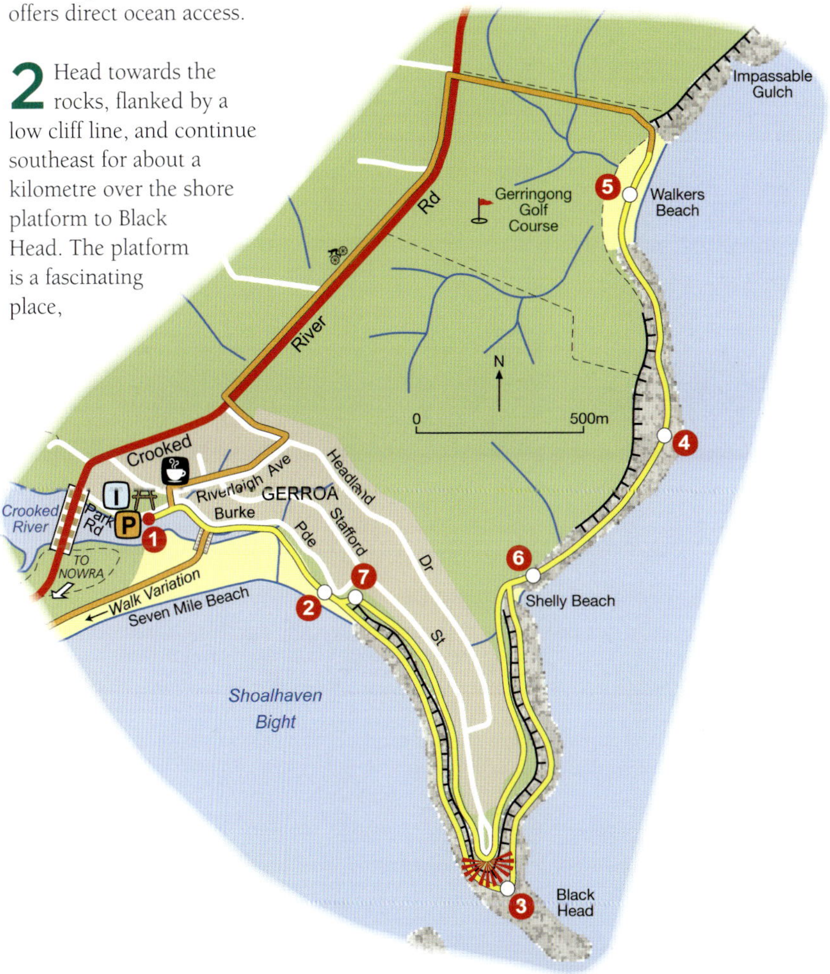

4 At lowish tide this headland is not difficult to negotiate but there's a little boulder-hopping to do at the northern end, just before the reddish sands of Walkers Beach are reached.

5 Secluded Walkers Beach is perfectly named and you're likely to have it to yourself even on a warm summer's day. It is fringed by lush farmland and the fairways of Gerringong Golf Course; views extend inland to Barren Grounds and Saddleback Mountain. A wide gulch past the beach's northern end prevents onward progress below the cliff line. If you want to while away time here and high tide prevents your return, there is a public easement or right-of-way along the northern boundary of the golf course to the road and a foot/bike path which provides a scenic 2.5-kilometre return through rolling farmland to Gerroa. Tide permitting, return the same

Walk variation – Seven Mile Beach loop

If you've energy to burn or you want to let the tide ebb before tackling the main walk, this 10-kilometre extension traverses the forest and beach of Seven Mile Beach National Park. Cross the footbridge over Crooked River and walk south for about 3 kilometres on Seven Mile Beach, turning inland to a beach access track and a viewing platform and boardwalk to reach the park's main picnic area (off Beach Road). A service trail leaves from the southwest corner; follow this south through giant eucalypts and burrawang palms. Back in the horse-and-buggy days, the Old Sand Track was the road from Gerroa to Shoalhaven Heads. With luck you might see or hear yellow-tailed black cockatoos or swamp wallabies. Veer left onto an old track for a few hundred metres to reach the beach for the long walk back to the footbridge.

way to the southern end of Shelly Beach.

6 Here a grass strip between the coast and a row of beach houses can be followed uphill back to Black Head Reserve. Walk to the rear left corner of the end house on Stafford Street closest to the reserve, then take the faint narrow footpad through scrub behind the property's backyard. Soon you'll emerge onto a narrow, grassy reserve which can be walked all the way back to Burke Parade at the northern end of Seven Mile Beach. You'll get good views down to the rock platform and over the beach to the south.

Seven Mile Beach

7 Either continue on the road or drop down to the beach sand to return to Emery Park. Close at hand is the award-winning Seahaven Café – definitely worth a stopover at walk's end!

Illawarra history – Charles Kingsford Smith

Perched near the top of Gerroa on Headland Drive, you'll find the Kingsford-Smith Memorial Lookout, commemorating the aviator who made the first flight from Australia to New Zealand. The long, broad and flat sands of Seven Mile Beach provided the perfect runway for the *Southern Cross's* takeoff to New Plymouth on 11th January 1933. Thus the trans-Tasman mail service began. Sir Charles was back later that year providing passenger flights from the beach.

Red Point, Port Kembla

TO SYDNEY
Helensburgh
TO WALK 1
Fwy
Hwy
Lawrence
Otford
Rd
Dr
Wakehurst
Lady
Otford
Darkes Forest
Princes
Southern
Hargrave
4
Stanwell Tops
Dr
Lawrence Hargrave Memorial Park
Stanwell Park
See inset below
Darkes
Forest
Rd
3
Dharawal Nature Reserve
10
Hargrave
Coalcliff
Fwy
Lawrence
Clifton
Hwy
Scarborough
Maddens Plain
11
Wombarra
N
0
2Km
Princes
Dr
Coledale
Southern
7
TO WOLLONGONG
8
Hargrave
Austinmer
Lawrence
Thirroul
Princes
Point St
Dr
Dene
Cres
Ave
Chellow
The
6
9
Hargrave
Stanwell Park
Drive
Park
Pde
Railway
Station
St
5
Lawrence
Stanwell Ave
Park Reserve
Beach Rd

Lake Cordeaux
Mt Keira
Southern
Corrimal
East Corrimal
13
Fernhill
Hwy
12
Towradgi
Balgownie
Fwy
Mt Pleasant
Princes
Mt Keira
17
Rd
Keiraville
Wollongong North
See below
Wollongong West
Wollongong
Kembla Heights
Mt Kembla
Figtree
Coniston
18
19
Hwy
Cordeaux Heights
Mt St Thomas
0
2Km
N
Farmborough Heights
Fwy
Princes
Cringila
Southern
20
Berkeley
21
Warrawong
Port Kembla
Horsley
Dapto
Kanahooka
Lake Illawarra

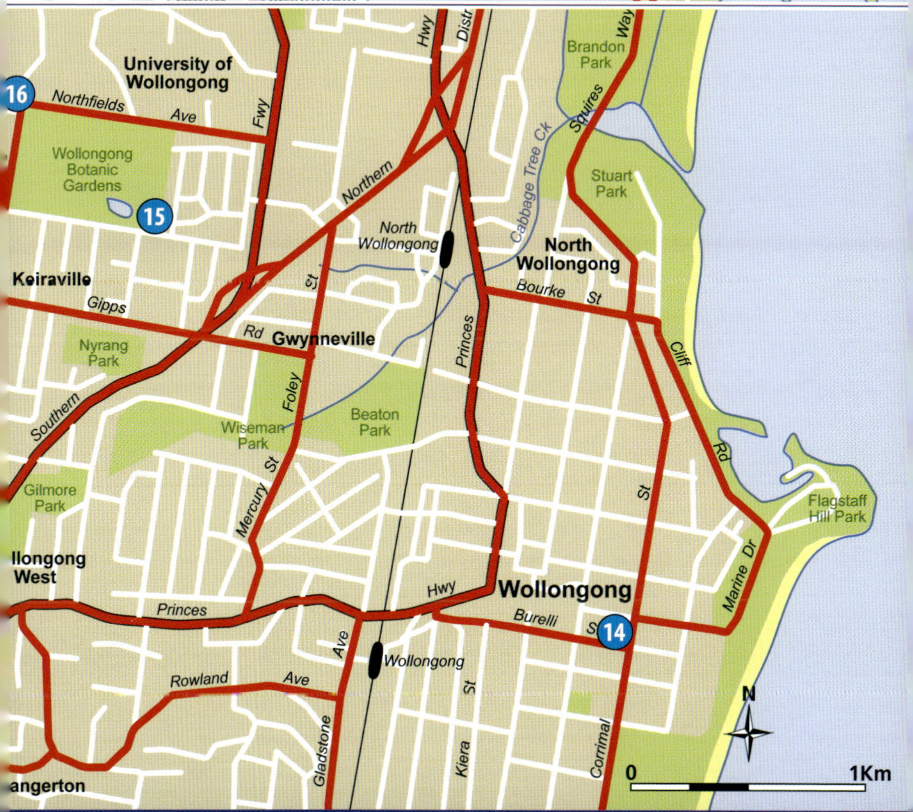
University of Wollongong
16
Northfields Ave
Fwy
Hwy
Distr
Brandon Park
Way
Squires
Wollongong Botanic Gardens
15
Northern
Cabbage Tree Ck
Stuart Park
North Wollongong
North Wollongong
Keiraville
Gipps
St
Bourke St
Rd
Gwynneville
Nyrang Park
Princes
Cliff
Southern
Foley
Beaton Park
Wiseman Park
Rd
St
Gilmore Park
Mercury
St
Flagstaff Hill Park
llongong West
Hwy
Wollongong
Marine Dr
Princes
Burelli
St
14
Ave
Wollongong
Rowland
Ave
St
N
Gladstone
Kiera
Corrimal
0
1Km
angerton

Kangaloon
Mt Murray
Calderwoo
Macquarie Pass National Park
Macquarie Pass
27
26
Illawarra
Robertson
Hwy
Illawarra
Jamberoo
Mountain
33
32
Knights Hill
Wildes Meadow
Carrington Falls
34
35
Budderoo National Park
30
Upper Kangaroo River
Brogers Creek
Kiama Harbour
Blowhole Point
Terralong
St
Bong
St
Bong
Noorinan
Collins
Kiama
Kiama
36
39
37
St
St
St
Barney
Shoalhaven
Farmer
St
Manning
St
Church Point
Kiama Surf Beach
Kendalls Point
40
Broughte Vale
Berry
Princ

Windang
Lake Illawarra
Haywards Bay
Princes
Lake Illawarra
Mt Warrigal
Rd
22
Barrack Point
Oak Flats
Illawarra Regional Airport
Shellharbour
Hwy
Shellharbour City
Illimbar
Albion Park
Hwy
Flinders
Shellharbour
23
24
Rd
Dunmore
25
Jamberoo
Curramore
38
Minnamurra
Hwy
29
Rd
Jamberoo
28
Kiama Downs
Jamberoo
Bombo
Rd
Jerrara
See inset opposite
Kiama
Princes
Kiama Heights
Saddleback Mountain
41
Foxground
Rose Valley
Werri Beach
42
Gerringong
Hwy
Toolijooa
Gerroa
43
N
0
5Km

Useful information

Visitors Centres

Southern Gateway Centre: Princes Highway, Bulli Tops, T 1800 240 737, www.visitwollongong.com

Shellharbour: Lamerton Crescent, T 4221 6169 or 1300 656 169, www.tourismshellharbour.com.au

Kiama: Blowhole Point Road; T 4232 3322 or 1300 654 262, www.kiama.com.au

National Parks

NSW National Parks and Wildlife Service
T 1300 361 967, www.nationalparks.nsw.gov.au

Transport

Green's Northern Coaches: T 4267 3884, www.greensnortherncoaches.com.au

Premier Illawarra buses: T 4272 1132, www.premierillawarra.com.au

Kiama Coachlines: T 4232 3466, www.kiamacoachlines.com.au

Rail information: T 131 500; www.131500.com.au

Free Gong shuttle bus: T 131 500; www.131500.com.au

Walking clubs

National Parks Association is a state-wide bushwalking club with a branch in the Illawarra. www.npansw.org.au.
Email: illawarra@ npansw.org.au.

South Coast Bush Walkers is based in Wollongong and undertakes medium to hard walks throughout the Illawarra and beyond: www.bushwalking.org.au/~southcoast.

Walkers for Pleasure gather for easy to moderate walks, co-ordinated by NSW Sport & Recreation, out of Kiama, Wollongong and the Bulli district. T 4228 535, www.dsr.nsw.gov.au/active/whatson_walk.asp.

Illawarra Ramblers are affiliated with WEA and walk on weekends and also mid-week. PO Box 1231, Wollongong NSW 2500, www.illawarraramblers.com.au.

Useful books

Murni Dhungang Jirrar: Living in the Illawarra, 2005, Department of Environment & Conservation (about traditional Aboriginal uses of local natural resources)

Discovering Illawarra's Bushland on Foot by Alan Fairley, 1999, Envirobook

Flowers of the South Coast and Ranges of New South Wales by Betty & Don Wood, 1998, Wood's Books

A History of Wollongong edited by Jim Hagan & Andrew Wells, 1997, University of Wollongong Press

Illawarra Heritage edited by Stephen Dovers, 1983, Environmental Heritage Committee

Native Plants of the Sydney District by Alan Fairley & Philip Moore 3/e, 2010, Kangaroo Press

Rainforests of the Illawarra District by Kevin Mills and Jacqueline Jakeman, 1995, Coachwood Publishing

Understanding the Scenery: Royal National Park & Heathcote National Park by Bob & Ann Young, 2006, Envirobook

Walkers Beach

Illawarra Wildflowers

Grass tree
Xanthorrhoea

Tea-tree
Leptospermum

Rice flower
Pimelea linifolia

Flannel flower
Actinotus helianthi

Coast rosemary
Westringia fruticosa

Coral heath
Epacris microphylla

King orchid
Dendrobium speciosum

Bronze Bush pea
Pultenaea villosa

Paper daisy
Helichrysum

Drumsticks
Isopogon anemonifolius

Guinea flower
Hibbertia scandens

Christmas bell
Blandfordia nobilis

Coast banksia
Banksia integrifolia

Hairpin banksias
Banksia spinulosa

Waratah
Telopea speciosissima

Gymea lily
Doryanthes excelsa

Showy grevillea
Grevillea speciosa

Honeyflower
Lambertia formosa

Native fuchsia
Epacris longiflora

Pink swamp heath
Sprengelia incarnata

Ledum boronia
Boronia ledifolia

Dog rose
Bauera rubioides

Trigger plant
Stylidium lineare

Purple fan flower
Scaevola ramosissima

Rainbow lorikeet

Crimson rosella

Galah

King parrot

White-headed pigeon

Satin bowerbird

Laughing kookaburra

Superb lyrebird

Eastern whipbird

Superb fairy-wren

White-throated treecreeper

Eastern yellow robin

Silvereye

New holland honeyeater

Lewin's honeyeater

Eastern spinebill

Dusky moorhen

Purple swamphen

Masked lapwing (plover)

Black Swan

Sooty oystercatcher

Hooded plover

Little pied cormorant

Australian pelican

Index

Index

About the Authors

John and Gillian Souter have been keen walkers for many years and are the authors of *Best Bush, Coast and Village Walks of the Shoalhaven*. Previously, they have written three books on walking in Europe (*Classic Walks in Western Europe*, *Walking Italy* and *Walking France*) and *Slow Journeys*, an entertaining ramble over the pleasures and practicalities of walking. They are currently researching a book on walking in the Southern Highlands for Woodslane.

Acknowledgements

Thanks are due to Andrew Swaffer from Woodslane who trusted us with the project. John and Gwenneth Prior were extremely helpful and generous with ideas and information. Thanks too to friends who accompanied us on walks. We are also grateful for advice and suggestions from Pam Lunnon and Peter Kennedy from National Parks and Wildlife.

Fishermans Beach, Port Kembla

Photography and cartography

Thanks to the following for supplying photos: Brett Davis for the bottom photo on page 197; Michael Smith for the frog on page 186; Dennis Gray for the Illawarra Fly on page 148. All other photos were taken by Gillian and John Souter. All photographs are copyright © the authors or other photographers and may not be reproduced without permission.

All of the maps in this book were created by Tony Fakira. They are copyright © Woodslane Press and may not be reproduced without permission.

Woodslane Press

Best Bush, Coast & Village Walks of the Illawarra is just one of a growing series of outdoor guides from Sydney publishers Woodslane. To browse through other titles available from Woodslane, visit www.travelandoutdoor.com.au If your local bookshop does not have stock of a Woodslane book, they can easily order it for you. In case of difficulty please contact our customer service team on 02 9970 5111 or info@woodslane.com.au or order directly at www.travelandoutdoor.bookcentre.com.au.

Titles include:

Best Bush Coast & Village Walks of the Shoalhaven

$29.95

ISBN: 9781921683183

Sydney's Best Harbour & Coastal Walks

$29.95

ISBN: 9781921606274

Sydney's Best Bush Park & City Walks

$29.95

ISBN: 9781921203145

Best Bush & Coastal Walks of the Central Coast

$29.95

ISBN: 9781921606854

Blue Mountains Best Bushwalks

$29.95

ISBN: 9781921606243

Canberra's Best Bush, Park & City Walks

$29.95

ISBN: 9781921683381

Adelaide's Best Bush, Coast & City Walks

$29.95

ISBN: 9781921683350

Best River & Alpine Walks around Mt Kosciuszko

$29.95

ISBN: 9781921606045

Best Village & Coastal Walks of the Sunshine Coast

$29.95

ISBN: 9781921683237

Perth's Best Bush, Coast & City Walks

$29.95

ISBN: 9781921606793

Your thoughts appreciated!

We do hope that you are enjoying using this book, but we know that nothing in this world is perfect and your suggestions for improving on this edition would be much appreciated.

Your name ______________________________

Your address or email address ______________________________

____

____

Your contact phone number ______________________________

Are you a resident or visitor to the Illawarra? ______________________________

What you most liked about this book ______________________________

____

____

What you least liked about this book ______________________________

____

____

Which is your favourite walk featured in this book?

____

Which walk wasn't featured but you think should have been included?

____

Would you like us to keep you informed of other Woodslane books?
If so: are you interested in:

- ☐ walking
- ☐ visiting natural & historic sites
- ☐ picnicking
- ☐ cycling
- ☐ general outdoor activities
- ☐ activities in the Illawarra region only
- ☐ activities in NSW
- ☐ activities around Australia

What others books would you like to see in this series?

____

____

Woodslane Pty Ltd • 7/5 Vuko Place • Warriewood • NSW 2102
Fax: 02 9970 5002 • Email: info@woodslane.com.au